MY GIRLS

Katie And Kelly
Changed My Life

John Cunningham

Order this book online at www.trafford.com
or email orders@trafford.com

Most Trafford titles are also available at major online book retailers.

Note for Librarians: A cataloguing record for this book is available from Library
and Archives Canada at www.collectionscanada.ca/amicus/index-e.html

Printed in Victoria, BC, Canada.

ISBN: 978-1-4269-1977-0 (sc)

*Our mission is to efficiently provide the world's finest, most
comprehensive book publishing service, enabling every author to
experience success. To find out how to publish your book, your way, and
have it available worldwide, visit us online at www.trafford.com*

Trafford rev. 9/23/2009

 www.trafford.com

North America & international
toll-free: 1 888 232 4444 (USA & Canada)
phone: 250 383 6864 ♦ fax: 812 355 4082

Dedication

Did you ever think you could love something as much as your own child?
Anne Smith- Mother of Becky Hoech

This book is dedicated to my two girls, Kelly and Katie. I will always love you more than anything in this world. I would also like to thank all of the people who have made a difference in my life. A special thank you to my immediate family, who I am so thankful to have every day. To all of my former coworkers who taught me so much, I say thank you. To my friends, especially John Scott, Kevin O'Herron, Joe Palumbo, John Gaffney, Ken Luckadoo, thank you for always being by my side. Lastly, I ask everyone who reads this to visit www.liftupellie.com to read a special story about a special girl who needs our prayers and support.

Chapter 1

Kellie and Katie Saved My Life

June 1999. Driving down City Line Blvd in Philadelphia. The phone rings. It's my boss. I'd better get it.

"John it's Ira. How are you?"

"I'm good. Just heading to an appointment."

Ira doesn't need to know I'm so hung over I can barely move my head. But then again, why shouldn't I be hung over? I am 29, making $15K a month. I live in a one-bedroom apartment, my car's almost paid off, and I have no other debt. My job is going to offices and selling annuities. The stock market is booming, and I have lots of potential for more business. So I tell Ira I am doing great and tell him how hard I'm working.

Ira recently took a chance and promoted me, so I never want to let him down. Ira has some better news for me. He just received May's final figures and I'm going to make $30,000 dollars this month. $30,000 THOU-SAND dollars this MONTH. I'm happy, but still kind of numb from my previous night. Thanks for the good news Ira. This run will never end.

In 1998, I made $48K for the whole year. Now, I'm already well over six figures and it's only June. 1999 is going to be a great year. It has been so far. I have always been religious and always believe in helping the unfortunate, especially when my luck is at an all time high. When I realize how much money I am making, I grab for my checkbook and I write two checks. One check goes straight to my mother. I want her to have the best of everything in life and make her happy. She is in her late fifties and working so hard. My mother has a heart of gold and she is truly a role model for any mother. She would give anything for her children, and has done so many times in her life. I hope that one day I can reward my mother and spoil her with gifts, knowing that she would donate them to charity and ask me to take her to a nice dinner. Some people are so easy to please. My mother is one of them.

The other check goes to my Aunt Dorothy. She had an even harder life. Her husband is a gambler, lazy, and a deadbeat. Sorry, Aunt Dorothy, but your choices in men just weren't that great. I miss you a lot and I wish you could see my family now. You were a great Aunt.

1999 continues to go the same way. Month after month I see great results. I'm invited to so many parties for all the branches I'm covering. Damn, but I have so many black tie invites that I'm going to have to buy/invest in a tuxedo. Rentals – they're for people who don't make the kind of money I make. Buying a tuxedo is a real milestone in my life – almost a rite of passage.

The Christmas season of 1999 is one of the best I've ever had. I can buy expensive gifts for my family and all of my top producers, and not skip a beat. I can remember walking through the streets of Philadelphia, hearing the clinking bells of the sidewalk Santas, seeing all the lights. Now a tear comes to my eye and I take a brief pause. Here I am - a kid from New Jersey who had so much trouble with high school, college, and the NASD exams - going to make $242,000 dollars, and now all of this.

For a fleeting moment, I think about buying a real nice home and a great car instead of my two-door Ford Explorer. Then discretion slaps me back to reality. Keep the money in the bank and keep those mutual funds in check. Besides, technology is killing it now.

I hear the words in my head ...you're going to retire early kid.

Christmas comes and goes just like I thought. It's nice to have just a two hour drive to see the family. Making lots of money and driving such a short distance to see my four brothers and sister who all live in New York and New Jersey is such a treat. Oops, before I leave New Jersey, time to slip mom a couple hundred bucks. I love traditions and giving my mom a treat will be a constant tradition, or will it?

2000 started as great as 1999 ended.

I have now started having parties at my apartment to share my good fortune with my coworkers. I love these guys. They work so hard for me. I want to reward them. Why not cater in some great food and buy so much alcohol we can't drink it all? It is only money after all, and next month another commission check will top this one. Oops, time to write mom another check.

February begins a deep spiral that concerns me. My production is slipping and I'm hearing rumors that my boss in trouble. We've had a big organization change and I don't think the new boss likes my boss. I'm thinking they'll work this out and we'll go back to normal. I am not worried I tell myself. My brokers love me and the branch managers who truly matter are always on my side. Besides, I have a trip to a resort to plan. I love going to resorts because as a kid, I never went on a vacation. I was always at soccer camps or working on a farm. These resort trips are making up for lost opportunity.

I feel my stomach churning. Where did that come from? As I relax in one of the nicest beds I have ever slept in, I look up and wonder why in the hell my stomach's churning like it used to churn before a big game. It's Sunday, and I should be worried about my hangover and if I offended anyone last evening. I had a lot of beers. Got to work on controlling my drinking. My weight is at an all time high. But, there's always the distraction of doing what makes me feel good – checking my bank account. It's almost six figures. Life is good. Get some sleep, John,

I tell myself. You have to go horse back riding tomorrow.

Chapter 2

When I return to Philadelphia, things are getting strange. It's now the spring of 2000 and the rumors of changes are rampant. I got a phone call from the head of another business unit who told me to come to Jacksonville to meet him. I don't like this at all. Feels somewhat like cheating on your girlfriend, although I'm the last one to talk about girlfriends. I haven't had a girlfriend in two years. My financial advisors prefer to watch me get drunk and hit on girls. Why? I suspect it's because they want to live vicariously through me. They see me, some single guy with a boatload of money hitting on all the chicks, and I think they worship what they think is my love 'em and leave 'em lifestyle. Little do they know I am lonely and would love to be involved with a great partner. A girlfriend would hurt my popularity with them and I can't have that. Besides, the Fed is lowering rates and the market is slowing down. My technology funds better be okay.

I find out that the guy who is calling me is replacing Ira, my friend and mentor. Now this trip I didn't want to go on is a must. Not only do I have to go, I must tell him my loyalty is to the company and to him. Ira who? This was my first experience with office politics. I'd like to tell you it was my last, but that's not the case. Could this job not be my dream job? No way! I'm great at my job and my guys love me. This is just a bump in the road.

The Jacksonville trip goes well. Kevin seems like a nice guy, and I come away from our meetings feeling great. Although I hate that I know Ira will be fired before Ira knows, I need to look out for myself. I need to write my checks to mom and Aunt Dorothy. Farewell Ira. I never thought when you left, the beginning of the end would soon follow.

The changes had become obvious. We now had frequent conference calls and had to go to New Jersey to present our topics to our new boss as he sat there, seeming to almost enjoy watching us try to impress him. I'm not sure that I like this, but the money's still good, not great, and my financial advisors love me, or do they?

2000 is shaping up to be a good year, but not nearly what 1999 was. I find that I'm losing business to other companies I had never heard of before. Things are changing around me and I'm not the superstar I was a few short months ago. I probably should glance at my resume and reach out to Ira and other former coworkers. Nah, this is going to pass and I'll be fine. I will never be poor again. I will never be poor again. I will never be poor again. Yeah, right!

2000 comes to an end, and there is change all around me. Our regions are changing and my territory is now shifting. In the beginning of 2001, I receive a call with the news that after careful consideration, I will be relocated to Charlotte, NC. I've been to Charlotte a few times and it seemed nice, but do I really want to move to the south. This was a big mistake on my part. I never questioned why I was being moved, nor could I discuss my options with someone. I saw Ira get fired, and I didn't want to be next in line.

Looking back, I should have contacted my boss or his boss and asked what the reasoning behind this move was. I wouldn't have done it in a confrontational manner, but the point remains I should have done something. I was viewed as the single guy who would do anything to keep his job. One of my coworkers in Philadelphia was approached about relocating. He told the company no thanks. He had confidence and he had a great circle of friends in the industry he knew cared about him. I had neither and they knew it.

My resume is done and I have no other prospects for employment. Pack the car and get to route 85 south. It's time to be a southerner ...ya'all.

Chapter 3

As soon as I get to Charlotte, everything is changed. I get to my new *office*. It's no office, but a cubicle My mutual fund counterpart is behind me, but he's in a spacious office. This should have been my tip off that I wasn't very well thought of. When you sacrifice yourself to move five hundred miles away from home and there isn't an office for you and no one bothers to help you find an apartment, you are truly alone. Think Eskimo on an ice float alone. The problem was that I had received so many compliments in the past, I just thought back to those moments instead of thinking about what was going on right here and right now.

I miss Philadelphia.

It's now 2001, and my new territory and I are not clicking. My $5 million a month in volume is now $3 million, and going the wrong way. My checks are going down and I am lonely. I am in a one-bedroom apartment, and my friends are all back in Philadelphia.

Charlotte has a nice feeling to it, and I feel real safe at night. The people are so nice, and it's a very clean town. In fact, after a night of drinking, a walk home feels good. I don't miss a night of drinking and running home drunk like I did in Philly. Could this city be growing on me?

My first summer in Charlotte and wow is it hot. Spring comes in early March and summer begins in April, or so it seems. I now have a few good friends, and I'm starting to like my life a little more. The one thing I am struggling with is my volume. Every day, I see the sales reports and I want to crawl under them. I used to be top three out of twelve. Now, I am bottom three out of twelve. I need to find out fast what's going on.

I begin the true summer working as hard as I can. I plan a Tennessee trip in July. This is part of my new territory, and I need to bring my whacky single life to these guys. They will love me, I hope. It is July 9, and I head out to Memphis. The Memphis office is a top producing office. The manager greets me warmly, and I meet some nice people. He has three financial advisors who love annuities. I can't wait to see these guys. I wait outside their office for what seems like hours. I'm John Cunningham. Just let me in and let's do business already. Their assistant comes out and asks me what company I am with. She goes back into their office and come back out.

"Sorry" she says, "They thought you were with another company. We don't have time today, okay?"

Her cute southern accent aside, I'm pissed. Do you know who I am I'm thinking. I guess they didn't because I left without even giving them my business card. Are you kidding me? In the past, I didn't even knock on doors; I just walked in and said let's do business. Now I am waiting on people to open their doors. Times are changing and I don't like it. Well, time to get in my rental car and head to Nashville. It's a long drive and I will figure this all out soon enough. Mom needs a nice check and I need to get back into the top three.

Rumors are swirling that there may only be nine regions soon. The market is once again dropping and times are getting tough. Where's my rental Malibu? As I drive on Route 40, my thoughts are all about my father. I'm not sure if I am his favorite, but now that I am away from him, he's calling me and he now knows how to email. That is a shocker. I had to change the channels on the TV for him as a kid.

Why am I thinking about my father this whole drive? I am having flashbacks on how rotten he was to my siblings and how he could be so mean to my mother. These thoughts need to go away. I need to figure out how to get my boss's attention, and in a good way. I need a $5 million month and I need to get out of the bottom three. There are rumors that we will reduce to nine regions and right now I won't make the cut. Where is Nashville anyway? A hundred miles from here and I need to stop thinking about Dad.

The thoughts continue to swirl and now I just go with it. Why did I agree to go to a baptism with him this weekend? Two flights from Knoxville just to make Dad happy. This is crazy. I may call him when I get to my hotel. I need business not family events. Since I barely speak to my cousins, why should I go? But you know, I know I'll go anyway, so why fight it. Dad wants me there and I'm the only family member who will go with him. Thank goodness Nashville is almost here.

I don't know if you've ever thought about someone for three straight hours. Let me tell you that if you do, you wind up really reliving a good deal of your own life. I had a good childhood, but it wasn't great. I heard and saw my father do things that made me so nervous. I think I am a pleaser to this day because I wanted to always please my father or anyone I perceived as an authority figure.

I never saw anyone stand up to my father. He was a dictator in every way. He was the type of guy who would blast his wife and kids all morning and then go to church and sing like he was Pavarotti. It makes me sad to think about what he could have been in life and what he truly was. He made it a point to get his six children an education, no matter how broke he was. He would find the money for high school tuition, sporting camps, and Christmas gifts, but I never heard him say "I love you."

I hope that I take half of his parenting skills and I hope I never come close to having the other half. There is no room for abuse, whether it's physical or verbal. I lived a great deal of my life fearing his outbursts, although they were seldom directed at me. It makes me want to cry when I relive his antics. I think there are still some deep scars within my family.

Finally, I am at my hotel. As I open my hotel door, my cell phone rings. I glance down and see it is my mom and dad's house. What do these people want now? If it is my father asking about this baptism, I may tell him I am not coming once and for all. Get real I tell myself. You're going and you know it. You will never let your father down.

It's my younger brother and he doesn't sound good. He asks me if I'm alone. I know right away that this isn't a good question. He screams in the phone that Dad died today. After that, I don't remember much of anything. My father had a massive heart attack in New York City coming home from work. The whole night is a blur. I remember thinking what do I do, but there was no answer. My father was lying on a table somewhere in New York City, here I am in Nashville trying to get a flight out, and no one could help me. The next flight out wasn't until 10: 00 a.m. the next day. I had to sit in a hotel room all night by myself. Thank goodness my siblings all called me and we got to share our grief together. I called some friends, such as Joe Palumbo, who helped a great deal.

Any time I doubt my faith in God or my religion, I think back to July 10, 2001. If there isn't a holy spirit, there was something changing every one of my thoughts about my father. It was almost like my father was talking to me as he was dying, and he was coming into my mind loud and clear. I wish I had known he was in trouble. I would have told him loudly that I loved him. We went 32 years without saying those words, and I regret it.

I have never given anyone advice on pain or suffering. I don't feel as though I am qualified to do that. However, I will tell anyone that is listening to make sure you tell your parents how much you appreciate what they have done for you while they are alive. I said it many time to my father, but it was when he was in a casket.

Once it became too late to call anyone else, the pain began. The longest night of my life was July 10, 2001 and, unfortunately, more long painful nights were ahead of me. I just didn't know it.

The funeral came and went and, although it was painful, it was peaceful. I needed to know that my father knew I was coming to the baptism with him. My mother assured me he knew. I hope she was right. Someday, when my dad and I meet up in heaven, I can get closure on that. When I looked back at the funeral, the one thing that was missing to me was coworkers. My siblings all had friends and coworkers everywhere. I had one co-worker attend the viewing. The funeral was in New Jersey where my company was headquartered. After seven years, was I really that unpopular? Time will tell, and I hate to say the answer was yes.

My father was buried on a Saturday, and I flew back to Charlotte on Sunday. I always regret not spending more time to grieve with my family but, even during that painful time, I knew my job was now officially in jeopardy. When your boss or coworkers don't bother to come to the most shocking and painful event of your life, the handwriting is on the wall. Have I mentioned yet that corporate America was scaring me?

Chapter 4

2001 continued on and in July my numbers didn't get any better. I was working Saturdays and long evenings, but my volume was now at $2 million and my target number was $4 million. You don't have to be a mathematician to say Cunningham is in trouble. Although my counterparts weren't faring much better, they were ahead of me. Rumors and low numbers started my trend of sleepless nights. These nights continued for six grueling years.

    September 11, 2001 - I wake up feeling miserable. I didn't know how to improve my volume and, to make matters worse, my morning appointment had already cancelled. I went to the gym at my apartment complex. While working out, the TV interrupted with breaking news about an accident at the World Trade Center. An hour later, the truth had surfaced and the only concern I had was finding my brother who worked close to this tragedy. Thank God my brother surfaced, but many of our family friends didn't. This event put my father's death in perspective. Children lost parents who were younger than me by twenty years. I think this affected me for many months.

September 11 gave many sales people a bit more time to improve numbers because no sales manager wanted to pull the plug on someone after a national tragedy. This would change a few months later. I remember dragging myself to work when the markets reopened. It was hard, but as a nation we did have to go on. I can officially say that this was the beginning of the end of my run with my company. In 1994, I started as a young clueless boy. Now, it was looking like 2001 would be the end.

I got a small reprieve when two of my better advisors started sending me business in November. My volume peaked and I felt okay about things. Their favorite football team was heading to the Super Bowl, and they called to remind me how much business they did and asked me to get them Super Bowl tickets. Then, somehow, tickets also became flights and a hotel. But hey, what the heck. They were my saviors and they were going to help me in 2002. What I didn't plan on was that another sales person got them front row tickets to a heavy weight boxing match and suddenly my 2002 was all but dead. The lesson here all you young ambitious sales people is this: You can spend money and win people, but as soon as someone has deeper pockets, you are yesterday's news. When you target people to be your business partner, you should look for people who are interested in your product and not your budget. This was the most painful lesson I have ever learned in business. I spent over $4,000 on them and used all of my frequent flyer miles. In return, I got no business in 2002, and in the spring - I think it was March - I was officially terminated. I wasn't the only person terminated. In fact they never got called it a termination it was a reorganization. Or was it a downsize? There were others let go besides me, but I knew the truth. It was due to low volume.

My boss at the time didn't even have the guts to do it or call me and see how I was doing. He had some lady from human resources call me and the call lasted all of three minutes. Three minutes to say you are terminated and here is how you send us your laptop. The woman, who was very nice, also gave me my severance amount. Do you remember the line from Goodfellas? "A lifetime of service and all I got was a handful of money"? That's exactly how I felt. I was bitter and hurt, but a decent severance package did help my cause.

I learned so much from this experience, but I hate to say it wasn't all good. I did receive some phone calls from coworkers expressing sadness and offers to help me, which was nice. I never heard from the Branch Managers who I gave all of my budget money to or who I dined with, at my cost, over the years. The thing I learned from this is what college professors should teach every student in any business class. People in business are out for themselves and, as long as you are meaningful to them, you are in. If your product isn't exactly what they need, you are out. The only way to overcome an inferior product is to have extremely deep pockets. I didn't have either and I was shown the door. My own broker stopped sending me business, but he never reminded me that my technology fund was now at an all time low. It was also at this time that I realized that corporate America had a slight smell of greed. Or did it reek of it?

Now here is my situation. I live in a city where I have lived for only one year. I have no job, very few friends, and I am dazed and confused.

Chapter 5

I took April, May, and June off to gather myself and figure out my next move. Well, actually I had those months off because I didn't know what to do with myself. I was okay financially, but I hated not leaving my apartment in the morning. I remember one morning I went to get a newspaper. As I walked to my car, a neighbor who I barely knew asked me if I was unemployed. That is a rotten thing to say to someone, especially when you don't know them. I could feel butterflies or panic build in my stomach. I had almost a year to prepare for being unemployed, and I didn't have one thing going on for a new job. To all of you at home, if you think you are going to lose your job, act accordingly and make proactive inquiries to headhunters, friends, and former coworkers.

Although I wish I could say my time of unemployment was like George from Seinfeld's "summer of George," it wasn't. When you have worked since you were 12 years old, it is very hard to shut it down and not worry. I rarely slept, and alcohol was the only sleeping pill that remotely worked. I finally got an interview with a former competitor, and it seemed like a marriage made in heaven. The hiring manager was a graduate of my college, and the two of us hit it off on the surface. I accepted the job wholesaling annuity products for AIG Sun America. Big company, good name, I can do this. This is another incorrect statement on my part.

When I look back on my resume and I see AIG on it, I think about it the way a person looks at a former lover and says what was I thinking. I chose this job for all the wrong reasons. Young people, please do your homework. When selecting a company, look at what they offer the public. Is it a good product? Do they have good customer service? Can you see yourself working for your boss? If the answer is no to these questions, you have two choices. The first is to walk away and not accept the offer. The second choice is to accept the position and begin interviewing other places or begin interviewing because you will be getting fired.

I knew I had made the wrong choice in my first month when we were at a company event and the boss jumped on a table and began screaming the lyrics to the Queen song *we will, we will rock you*. I'm not sure about you, but if a grown man is standing on a table in Los Angeles yelling we will rock you to his employees, it isn't a good thing. As I boarded the plane to come back across the country, I thought to myself the boss is a lunatic with a napoleon complex, the product stinks, and I'm hearing our customer service stinks. Is this bad? Oh, I will find out just how bad. My professional life at this time was not exactly where I hoped it would be, but I had a blind date or a set up, whatever you call it, and I heard she was cute.

The date was just what I needed, a normal high school assistant principal from a great family and very beautiful. We hit it off rather well, and I could see a future with her. The part of my life I knew I had no future was with AIG. I really tried to wholesale their products. For those of you who don't know, any time you buy a mutual fund or any investment product from a financial advisor, there is normally a salesperson selling that product to your advisor. For those of you who don't know this, the competition is fierce. For every mutual fund you know about, there are thousands you don't know about. When financial advisors make a name for themselves as successful, generally grossing $250,000 a year or more, they get a few things such as good paychecks, a bigger office, and they get wholesalers who will do anything for their business. If you have ever gone to a financial advisor and bought mutual funds or an annuity, chances are your advisor was taken out for a nice dinner or maybe more.

As I mentioned earlier, I did my share of no no's such as Super Bowl trips, so I am no angel in this department. What I couldn't believe is how my Super Bowl gift was small potatoes compared to my competition. I was driving all over the Carolinas begging for business and I was losing to the higher bidder many times. Don't forget. I didn't have the best product, but it wasn't the worst either. Let me rephrase that they wanted me to beg for business I think I asked for it professionally.

I was in trouble and I refused to acknowledge it. Herein lies the lesson. If you have bad results two times in a row, begin taking stock in what is going on. Don't blame the product, management, or marketing teams. When you don't produce, sit back and ask yourself what is going on here. I was with two of the biggest companies in the world and failed twice. Although I had earlier success at Prudential, you must score yourself on your most recent report cards or, in the business world, by your w2s. If you have two consecutive negative endings, you must ask yourself if you are cut out for this. Ask yourself if people want to do business with you. Find customers you like and ask them bluntly if your competition is better than you. Ask them about your competition (what they do that you don't do) and ask them if you should be doing things differently. You have nothing to lose if you ask these questions. I never did that, and I regret it until this day.

So, you would think at this moment I was looking at other options and companies. Well, you'd be wrong. I thought I could make it work. I wanted to make it work. How can you tell if you are a bad salesperson? Here is an answer. I had arranged a luncheon at a big office in

Uptown Charlotte. I catered in lunch, paid ten dollars to park, and wore my nicest suit. This was a chance to get sales, build relationships, and win business. If need be, I thought, I could buy some sporting tickets and be a team player. I prayed to God prior to the meeting for business. Again, not a good idea. If you find yourself praying for business, I strongly recommend that you evaluate your career choice. I'm Catholic and I truly love God, but I just feel with a war going on, people losing their homes, and so much hatred, God doesn't have the time to look over your business plan and assist you.

Anyway, I was ready for my meeting. I presented to the group, handed out materials and business cards, and the group had two very important questions for me. The first question floored me. Do you want to play goalie for our men's soccer team? I'm fighting for my professional life and someone recognized me from a previous soccer league. The sad part was that I said yes and joined the team. I never received a dime in business, but I did get a concussion one game. The second question should have made me resign on the spot and look at a different career path. Do you know any good Ford Explorer mechanics? I see your key chain is that of an explorer?

This was the day from hell. I had worked so hard. I truly believed I had a plan and I was going to get the business I so desperately needed. Five hundred dollars down the drain and, to make matters worse, there was a message on my cell phone from my boss asking me to call him right away. That was an awful day.

To answer my original question, that's how you can tell you are a bad salesperson. If you can't make an impression on over twenty-five sales people or even get a promise of I will look at your product in the future, it's time to think and act fast. Looking back, I now disagree with my belief that I was a bad salesperson. I visited an office that had longstanding relationships with other sales people, and I didn't have what they wanted. It is so easy in sales to get down when people don't want your product.

The biggest mistake you can make is to compare yourself to other sales people in your company. If you want to compare, then compare yourself to other sales people who have been in your role for the same amount of time. It always makes me angry when bosses put out a production report each day and include the new people. Give them a break. You have so much to learn as a new sales person. The last thing you need is undue pressure from a boss who likes to embarrass those lagging in sales. For the record, hey bosses, we know when our sales suck. It shows in our paycheck.

Speaking of bosses, when I called mine back, he was very nice. He asked me what I was doing and how it was going. For traveling sales people, let me tell you a little secret. Your manager measures you on two things. The first is your sales. Numbers don't lie If your goal each month is $4 million and you hit $4 million or higher, your boss doesn't care what you are doing as long as it is ethical. Translation: do what you have to do to get the sale, as long as what you're doing doesn't get the boss fired. The second measurement is how many appointments are you going on and is your calendar full each month, so your boss can show this to his/her boss. Here is the last part of this secret. Your sales numbers better be at goal by month six or the second part is a moot point and you will be replaced.

My sales numbers were awful, but my boss knew I was hustling each day. In fact, there wasn't anyone on my team who was hitting goal. As we were about to hang up, I felt pretty good about our call until he said the words that struck me like a ton of bricks - well okay, get it going soon and you are now on warning. Was I in high school? No, I was in the real world and I was just told in no un-certain terms that I was just about out of gas. Did I listen this time? NOPE!

Chapter 6

The strange part about all of this was that I didn't care this time. For some reason, in past years I would have sat down, drawn up a business plan, and made a hundred phone calls to beg for business. However, this wasn't the past; it was the present. I took Kelly to a nice dinner and I expensed it. Sorry, AIG, it had to be done. The next month, I really was in a daze. I worked and went out on appointments, but I knew it was over. My boss called me out of the blue and told me he was coming to Charlotte and was going to travel with me for two days. I knew this couldn't be good, but deep down I knew I was a true sales person and I would show him what I could do.

Now I hadn't seen him since he was stomping we will rock you on a table, so I had no idea what he was going to be like to travel with. I can honestly say this was the longest and most bizarre two days of my life. To my readers entering the business world and who want to do sales, please take note here. When your boss comes into town and you pick him up at the airport, be ready for anything. I wasn't. When your boss gets in your car and starts looking around and snooping in your glove box, you should become afraid. But most importantly, when your boss travels with you, have an agenda ready and have appointments scheduled all day long. I didn't and I paid the price dearly.

We visited our first office together and when we arrived, I took out my bag loaded with marketing material ready to sell, sell, sell. I was going to show my boss I could do this job and I was going to ask for and get business that day. The first thing my boss did was rip my bag off of my shoulder and say I hate when my people lug things into an office. Two feelings hit me at that moment. First, fear. I had self doubt and my confidence was shattered. The second was to curl up my fist, throw a left hook, and let him find his own way back to the airport. I let the first win and I followed him like a puppy dog. The takeaway here folks is simple. Do your homework on your boss. Call coworkers and ask them prior to your boss coming to see you what to expect. Had I done that, my car would have been cleaner, my bag would have been home, and I would have been relaxed to sell.

After an unproductive no sale afternoon, I really felt like Adrian in Rocky screaming "stop the fight." It was time to end this misery, but instead I kept going because

Kelly was coming over to my house once I put this tyrant to bed. I had survived the first day with him and actually made one or two good presentations. Although he wouldn't say it, I know he thought it. So one more day and he heads back up north. How bad can one day be? Oh a lot worse and it would spell the end. Where should I take Kelly to dinner?

The next day we went to an office that just stunk. I will never mention names, but these guys were the worst stock brokers I have ever seen. Now granted, it's 2003 and the market wasn't strong, but this place was a graveyard. This was totally my fault. When planning sales appointments, plan to see the best. Never ever go to an office just because they will see you or you need to fill your calendar. If an office says you can come in tomorrow and give us a sales presentation, please stay away. That goes for any industry and any type of sales position. If an office can see you tomorrow, it means no other sales person bothers going there and there is a good reason for that.

Well, anyway, here how this story goes. I had everyone come into a conference room for a breakfast meeting so I could tell the AIG story. It wasn't a bad story; just not a great one. As I began, I thought I actually saw a grown man crying in the back of the room. It couldn't have been my presentation. I hadn't started yet. It was the market. It was terrible.

I finished my presentation, and everyone left the room except my boss. He waited until the door shut and ran at me. Now mind you, I am five foot ten at best, but he was like five foot five. He ran at me like a baseball manager runs at an umpire after a lousy call. He screamed in my face the words *just who (emphasis on who) do you work for?* I answered AIG. He screamed at me that I mentioned it once (that's right, only once) in my presentation. Here was this man looking up at me screaming and getting red in the face. I truly thought he wanted to fight me. Me, I'm a college graduate. I know I am not the best sales person in the world, but not close to the worst. At that very moment I was defeated and deflated.

Please remember this. Don't let anyone bring you down this badly. If your boss is abusive or just stupid, let them know it on the spot. It may cost you your job, but I can tell you that this moment cost me a lot more inside because I didn't fight back. I should have told him to take his bald, height challenged frame out of my face. What I did come to realize months later was that I was a very good sales person and I should have let him have it good. That is a regret I will have forever. To make matters even worse, my second appointment cancelled on me and we had nowhere to go. We went to the South Park Mall and stared at each other, barely speaking. We parted ways that afternoon and the job search was on full force. We parted ways in more ways than one. Shortly after our encounter we both made the decision to end our relationship. I knew I couldn't work for him and vice versa. I am not sure who ended the relationship officially but I know I watched a few weeks of law and order on their dime. Af-

ter learning what AIG did to the public a few years later
I wish I had watched more.

Chapter 7

I have been unemployed before, so this is no big thing to me. Besides, a recruiter in Florida had called me to tell me that Guardian Life was hiring and they wanted me on their team. This wasn't too bad. I received a small severance, a little time off; and my girl Kelly and I were getting closer. Let's rock. Here is my regret. I may have taken time off, but I never took stock off what had just happened to me. I had lost my job twice in a year and a half. What had I learned from all of this? Not a thing. You will lose your job in life if you work for big companies.

Look around today. Mortgage companies, banks, no one is safe. If you don't believe me, ask a person who worked for Enron. There was a bank recently that laid off five hundred employees due to the credit and mortgage collapse. That doesn't bother me. We all know it can and will happen from time to time. What truly bothers me is the CEO of the bank received close to $85 million last year in total compensation. How can someone sleep at night knowing that they have five hundred employees going home to tell their loved ones they are unemployed while they are living a lavish life? I truly believe that CEOs should be compensated for their leadership and experience. Is there a huge life style difference between $85 million and $60 million? I bet the difference could have saved hundreds of jobs. I will never bank with that institution again for that reason.

I have to stand up for the little people. I am one of them. I'm waiting for a CEO one day to stand up and say we are going to avoid layoffs because all of senior management who earn over one million are going to forfeit salary until this matter clears up. Greed is so prevalent it makes me sick.

The mistake I made is one I feel so many people make. I didn't take anything away from these companies that would make me a better employee in the future. If you are working for a company, take advantage of any training they offer that you feel will benefit you in another company or industry. If your company offers systems training, public speaking, time management, etc, do it. If you have the time and your company is willing to foot the bill for it, you are foolish not to take advantage of it. In fact, if you are employed now, go onto www.monster. com and look at another companies' hiring ads. If you see skills required that you don't have, please go get them. Make yourself better. If your company offers you tuition assistance and you don't take advantage of it, you are really leaving something on the table. I feel that tuition assistance is as valuable as a 401k match. For those of you who don't have children and can go out at night or watch TV for hours on end, go back to college and get your master's degree. Time is so important and, if you use it wisely, you can pick which companies you want to pursue, not vice versa.

If someone is offering to help pay your way, it is a crime not to take them up on it. In fact, you will thank me for doing it. I wish I had time to get my Master's degree. My brother received his MBA while working full time. His company paid a large portion of it. He is no longer with that company, but he will always have his MBA and he is kicking butt. Good for you, Tom. The lesson is simple. Take anything away from your employer that you possibly can. At some point, an executive at your company will make a mistake that will cost hundreds of people their jobs. If you think I am wrong, ask people at Bear Sterns, Bank Of America, Wachovia, HSBC, New Century, etc. how they are doing right now. These people were following orders and they are now paying the price. You can't help getting laid off. You can help yourself a great deal if you have more skills than anyone on the unemployment line. I still can't use power point to this day, and it makes me mad. The same goes for snag it.

Chapter 8

Well it's official. I am in love with Kelly and she is a great girl. She thinks I am a little nuts with all the job changes, but I will make Guardian a ten year gig and we will live happily ever after ... or maybe I won't. Kelly and I begin looking at wedding rings and all the things that go with that. Kelly and I get along very well, and she understands my job and knows that there are times when I won't be around due to business travel. It is so important to have someone who respects what you do and never makes you feel guilty for not being around. I truly think the distance between us in the beginning of the relationship helped to make us grow as a couple.

Kelly has and always will have her own life and that is great. I could never be with someone who solely depends on me for her social schedule. Kelly has her friends, her volunteer activities, and so much more to keep her happy. Hurray for me. This is the right woman and I know it. I am not one to give advice on dating or relationships, but I will say this. When a relationship is easy and you can be yourself and you constantly look forward to the next date, you are in a good one. Kelly gives me great support, lots of laughs, and she is quite easy on the eyes. Kelly and I can have a good time at a nice restaurant or watching reruns of a sitcom. We have never had any major fights and that's the way I like it. I fight all day for business. I truly don't want it in my personal life.

Picking out a ring for Kelly was a lot of fun, but also nerve racking. It is something she will wear forever and truly symbolizes what she means to me. I tried to plan a perfect engagement. That was a big mistake. I tried to have a night that was a flashback to our first date, something romantic, and something that involved her family since she is so close to them. The restaurant went okay except for the fact that I asked for the table we sat at on our first date. We got the table, but when Kelly went to the rest room, the staff brought champagne.

I hadn't communicated properly that I needed the table just to sit at and have an appetizer. The engagement would come later. The problem was I hadn't asked her yet and I had to chase them away. The proposal was to take place on a horse and carriage ride in uptown Charlotte. I went to a horse stand a week earlier and set up the time. Kelly was very suspicious of the evening, probably because I was acting like a fool. When we got into the car to head uptown, I noticed it was raining. We arrived at the location and there was a small problem. There was no horse and carriage. I had told Kelly we were meeting business friends, but she knew on Fridays I didn't have appointments.

I left Kelly in the bar where we were supposed to be meeting people, and called my horse guy. Is it a jockey? Well, anyway, he told me very politely that horses don't go out in the rain. *Horses don't go out in the rain?* Funny, but I've seen them in the Kentucky Derby run – *in the rain* - like champs. I guess I was wrong. The sad part was that I had no plan B and for one obvious reason I had to propose to her that evening.

This night was getting worse by the minute. I called a car service and was able to get a driver in a nice car to pick us up. We both love the look of St. Patrick's Cathedral in Charlotte. I figured I would propose on the steps of the Church, and it would still be romantic. We arrived at the Church, and I was feeling very nervous. I had two errors so far, and this night was becoming a mess.

As we arrived at the dark church, I told the driver we would be right back. Kelly was probably second guessing her choice in men right now, and was wondering if she still had her little black book. Who could blame her? Finally, we reached the top of the steps and I was ready to tell her I loved her and I wanted her to marry me. As I began my sermon, Kelly's eyes became as big as saucers and she looked over her shoulder. Yep, right there in the middle of what was supposed to be the most romantic moment of our lives stands the limo driver.

"I didn't know where you wanted me to be," the limo drive blurted out.

Pointing to the car, I told him "well, there would be a good start."

Three mistakes in thirty minutes. I should have been sent to single A for this performance. Finally, with our distraction gone, I asked her and, ta-dah … drum roll please, she said yes. Now what do we do? I had a cooler ready for this horse guy, but I couldn't bring a cooler into a car in which we were supposed to be going to a dinner meeting, so I had nothing. I asked the driver to stop at a liquor store, and he promptly took us to an Eckerd Drug store. How romantic - not.

Four mistakes and still counting. At this point, it didn't matter. I needed a drink, so we settled on Coors beer. Kelly was adamant about calling her family in Raleigh to share her news. There was a problem with that. They were all at her house with her roommate, Jennifer Sullivan, waiting to surprise the newly engaged couple. Kelly couldn't reach any family member, which was odd because her parents were home most evenings.

When we reached her home, she wouldn't go inside because she didn't want her roommate to find out before her Mom and Dad. After begging her for twenty minutes, she finally relented and decided to go into her house. As we were walking in, I noticed something in her bushes. Her boss, Nancy Bartles, and her husband Carl were late to the party and were hiding in the trees. That was the first time I laughed that evening. Kelly opened the door and her whole family was there to greet her and congratulate her. Finally, something went my way that night and made it special for my girl. I had to propose that evening, and people came from all over to share in it.

I knew it had been a brutal evening when I woke up the next morning and found two full beer bottles in my pockets. I was hiding beers at the party so I could keep drinking to settle my nerves. How pathetic is that. I wouldn't trade that night for the world. My girl said yes and we were planning a wedding.

Chapter 9

Guardian was a smaller company that had a good reputation for annuities with great fixed rates. They made me a good offer and my boss seemed like a good person. He was Catholic, he was an usher at the church, and he seemed to like me. Does this sound familiar? I made the same mistake twice in a year. I never called anyone to get any background on my boss. I knew people who worked at this company and, because all I wanted was a job, I signed on the dotted line.

For those of you at home now looking for work, let me tell you something. It is okay to be unemployed. It is okay to sit out and hunt for the right opportunity. If you do the right thing with your money when you make it, you earn that right. This is one of my biggest regrets in my professional life. The stigma of saying I was unemployed was too much for me. I just went to work for any company that offered me a job. You don't work for a company. You work for two people when you are in sales. You work for yourself and you work for your boss. You must manage your schedule, your sales, your efforts, and you must manage your boss. If you don't do that, you will never succeed. You must know at all times what your boss wants to see and hear. Whether it's a joke to you is not important.

North Carolina is a right-to-work state. That translates to this. You can be fired at any time and any place. You must know your bosses and know them well. If they want call reports, you must provide them. You signed on for it. Do your research prior to signing the contract. I don't mind working. In fact, I enjoy it.

During my first few weeks at Guardian, my boss was great. I mentioned earlier that Guardian had great fixed rate annuities. Annuities are like CDs, except you don't have to pay taxes until you take out the money. Well, let me tell you this. You have no way of predicting the future in life or I would have won the power ball by now, so I am not to blame here - well not totally.

I was at Guardian all of two weeks when the company announced that they were suspending fixed annuity specials. No wonder the person who had the job prior to me bolted. He must have had inside information. That brings me to a point. If someone approaches you about a great job with great earning potential, ask yourself why me. Why would anyone leave that job if it is so darn good? You have to be creative in how to ask that question, but if you get established in an industry, you should be able to gather that information. Of course, never ask that question during the interview process. Remember the old expression if something is too good to be true? Just be aware of what is said during an interview and research it.

Well, now here is my first Guardian appointment.

"Hey Guardian guy, what is your annuity special this month," an older gentlemen asks me.

"Sorry, but we no longer have one" I replied.

"Well, then, what are you doing here" he asked me.

We didn't have an annuity special, our mutual funds were average, and the 401k product was average. Here we go again, I'm thinking. Ladies and gentleman, I am proud to say three companies later I took the offensive. I started interviewing that month. I was on a good guarantee, but I learned the lesson.

It was 2004, and the markets were stabilizing pretty well. I had an interview with a good mutual fund company. Now, as I have moved around, my resume has gone from one page to two pages. Remember when I said earlier to sit out until you have the right choice? Here is why that became important. The women interviewing me said five times during the interview that she didn't think she could get past that I worked for three companies in three years.

As she was about to say it for the sixth time, I stood up and said, "I will make this easy for you. I am not apologizing for my past. Things happen. I had to work, and I made mistakes. Have a great afternoon".

It probably wasn't my shining moment as a professional, but I knew I didn't have a snowball's chance at that job, and I was tired of getting pushed around. I wasn't going to get that job, but I also wasn't going to leave my dignity in that interview room. Speaking of which, when you get the feeling you are tired of being pushed around and you are developing an attitude, I think that's a good thing. This woman was making me feel as though I didn't belong in that interview room with her. Well, not only did I belong in that room, she should have hired me. I didn't go to high school, college, and work so hard to be a pushover. Develop the attitude early. Don't be too aggressive, but don't take crap. I think when you are respected, it feels so good. She probably didn't respect me because I never did hear from her.

Guardian was actually going well, but I wasn't coming close to hitting my numbers. The good thing was that no one else on my team was either. In fact, no one in the company was doing great, so I knew I had time. I had a strong relationship with my boss and people around me were leaving left and right. My boss didn't have the time to bother me because he was always interviewing. Another easy sign. You need to get your resume out to employers. If you see high turnover in your company, it's time to ask what is going on here.

My car now had 84,000 miles in two years on it, and I never drove on weekends. These trips to South Carolina and the Virginias were long and getting old fast. One of my previous bosses said something to me back in 2001 that made a lot of sense. If you are a traveling sales person, you take your life into your hands every day. Get the most out of your job. I think he meant to have fun and stay in decent hotels. I take it this way. If you are traveling, whether it is by air or car, you must make the most money you can. If you are doing it and it isn't producing results, don't travel to that location anymore. Keep great records and focus on the places you do make money. This may sound elementary to some of you, but I didn't learn it for many years.

I wanted to have the best milk run of any sales person. By that, I mean I wanted a travel schedule that showed my boss that I could and would go everywhere for business. I wanted to turn in expense receipts from every state to show my bosses I was traveling and working. What I was doing was wasting time and increasing my odds of being in an accident. Traveling is great and can be fun. Just make sure you control where you go and, most importantly, why you go. Create notes after every overnight trip and document the results.

Be honest with yourself, but don't always be honest with your boss. As I said earlier, you have to manage your boss and here is why. A coworker at Guardian who was also a good friend and a damn good salesperson wore his heart on his sleeve. One day, our manager called him and asked him how his day was going. He replied honestly, telling his boss that two of his appointments cancelled on him, some guy who promised him business didn't come through, and some guy yelled at him because of the company's service levels. In other words, he told his boss he was having an awful day.

He did nothing wrong here, at least not among friends who are just venting. Where he made his mistake was who he told. You might think we are in this together and we can vent to our coworkers, boss, or non-boss. Not true. Two hours later the boss called him and told him he that he didn't like his attitude earlier. He went on to tell my coworker that if he copped that attitude in the field, he'd never get any business and how "concerned" he was about the guy's future at Guardian. Once again, the reminder here is please know everything about your boss, including knowing what you can and can't say.

He should have called me and vented. Our boss wore Guardian clothing all weekend long and wanted his life to be Guardian. He would have defended his company to the death. In fact, he's still there last I heard. You know who isn't there? My friend was terminated a month later. He was deemed to have a bad attitude. He didn't have a bad attitude at all. He wanted to win at all costs. He wanted to be able to say if we had this product, we can kick butt. If we had better service, people will use our products. Please let management handle issues like that. When a customer calls you with concerns about your products or services, please tell them one thing. Tell them you wish they would tell your boss.

The only way you should handle complaints about

your company is to tell your customer to express it for you. Your customer will respect you, and most times will pick up the phone or drop an email on your behalf. The best line to use is "I want to do business with John. I wish your company had this or that." If it is a service complaint, tell them to email you their complaint. You can then forward the email to your boss and ask nicely how we should handle this. Always give your boss the impression you are a team player and you have a positive attitude. If you call your boss angry about service or a product, they will view you as a troublemaker and your days will be numbered. I have seen this so many times in both industries.

The experience of my friend really shook me up. I was going to miss him, but most importantly I felt the same way that he did. The handwriting was on the wall. I had to get out and I had to do it before my guarantee expired. You see, folks, as time went on I learned lessons just a little slower than those around me. My boss and I continued to have a decent relationship on the surface. If I really told him how I felt or what I was thinking, I would have been shown the door as well.

I decided that if I wanted to have a successful marriage, I had to slow down the traveling. I put my resume everywhere and anywhere. One day, I got a call from a woman at HSBC about a marketing job for a mortgage company. I went to the interview. I was actually late to it because I knew nothing about mortgages and this didn't sound like anything I wanted to do, so I didn't give it the old college try. I interviewed with a man by the name of David Schroeder. I was immediately impressed with him and his demeanor. I told him straight out I knew nothing about mortgages and was not a marketing guy, but we talked for two hours anyway. We discussed sales ideas, which is my favorite topic, and success stories. We ended the interview and I thought it went well. He thought the same thing, and about a month later I was heading up a marketing team of four people. I resigned from Guardian two weeks after my honeymoon.

Guardian was so good at receiving resignations that it didn't faze anyone. Remember earlier when I told you to develop skills at your current employer? Well, this is where that lesson was learned. I can sell, I can email, I can present. I can't use Photoshop, power point; snag it, or any other software tool. This became a problem and it really never endeared me to my team. We all worked together, but the marketing team never functioned well. There were many reasons for that and I take the blame for a great deal of it. The lesson I learned here is simple. Ask exactly what your role will be in an interview. Try to develop a mental picture of what you will be doing and who will be reporting to you. Roles change constantly in business, but if you can get an idea of what you will be doing on a daily basis, you shouldn't have major surprises.

I think David and I liked each other so much we figured we could overcome any obstacle. We couldn't overcome all of our obstacles, but since Decision One

Mortgage was part of HSBC and was such a great company, I transferred to a sales role within the company. David Schroeder supported my transfer and guided me along the way. When you have someone in your corner, it makes life so much easier.

Chapter 10

A great wife, a good job, good friends, and a healthy family are all I ever wanted in life. Finally, it seemed as though I had them all. I wasn't making the money I had in the past, but we were okay and my new job looked awfully promising. People around me at HSBC were making $250k and up. I can do this; I know I can. 2005 was going to be a great year. By the way, I forgot to mention I was going to be a father. Kelly was pregnant, and we were ecstatic. This is the hardest part to write about but, for you folks taking business notes, I have to include this in the book.

I was an inside sales person. That meant I would be doing very little traveling. All of my work was done via phone, email, and fax. If I could make a good salary and be home every night and meet my wife for lunch occasionally, this would be a dream job. I started off a little slower than I thought, but we were all very confident. By we, I mean my sales manager Ken Luckadoo and his boss Mike Vowell. They were great guys and good friends and are still both to this day. They wanted me to produce, and so did I of course.

All I had to do was get mortgage brokers to send me their loans for people with bad credit. Subprime mortgages were everywhere and Wall Street was buying them in bunches. My territory was Memphis and a little bit of Mississippi. I immediately noticed that mortgage brokers weren't the most educated people and they seemed quite rude at times. Well, actually, all of the time. They wanted their loans closed when they said and always fought with you over the rate. I had twenty-five broker shops I could work with. Of the two shops that I had, I can honestly say that two people were smart and weren't constantly breaking the law. Sheila Lipman and William Strauss were the two I wish I could have dealt with every day because they were good people. The rest of my customers are the reason the mortgage industry is in shambles. They were liars, thieves, and bad people.

In order to do business as a stock broker, you must pass several difficult exams, and there are strong checks and balance systems in every office. In the mortgage industry, you needed very little in terms of licenses and there was no one there to supervise the process. We are currently in a crisis for a reason. We brought this on ourselves. Someone once told me there was no exam or a background check to be a loan officer in Colorado. That is sad. Be that as it may, I had a job to do and my job was to bring in loans and get them closed. Each day, I dealt with people who were lying about their clients' income or worse. When I say worse, I mean constructing w2s in their office or paying appraisers cash to lie about home values.

HSBC did as good a job of catching fraud as they could, but we all knew there were problems coming, or at least I did. If anyone ever wants to hear the inside stories of the mortgage business, please email me and I can give you all the horror stories that have never been told. The goal of an account executive was to have $3.5 million funded in loans or loans closed each month. If you did that, you would make about $200k a year. If you couldn't do $3.5, you had to hit $2.5 to have a decent paycheck, or about $125k a year.

Your month was so important that you worked all day bringing in loans you could close to get that volume to $2.5 or higher. The end of the month was the most stressful because as each elapsed, we worked with under-writers and account managers to do anything to have our loan close. In late March, I was at $2.3, but something worse was happening. Kelly had developed some light bleeding and we ultimately lost the baby. Now I am never one to ask for sympathy from anyone. In fact, after my father died, I never spoke about it while I was on sales calls for that very reason.

I wanted business for the right reason. Kelly and I

comforted one another, and I took a day off from work. When I returned to work, one of my loan officers named Bo called me and told me he had heard the news about Kelly. We had a mutual friend that had told him. I didn't mind people knowing about it. In fact, it helped to talk about it since whenever I looked at Kelly and saw the pain in her eyes, I knew we couldn't talk to each other about it. I needed to talk about it with friends and family. Bo was very kind and said some nice things to me. Most importantly, he had a $300k loan with me that would put me over the $2.5 mark and allow my wife and me to drive to the beach with a good feeling financially.

As Kelly and I were driving to the beach, we made a gas station stop. This was in the good old days when gas was slightly higher than three dollars a gallon. As I came out, I decided to call Bo and check to make sure his loan closed properly. A good salesperson will stop at nothing to satisfy his customers' needs and to make sure his customers are getting great service. Remember when I said earlier that this is hard? Here is why this part is hard for me to this day to tell. Bo picked up his phone. He sounded different. I asked him if the Jones loan went okay. After stuttering for a few moments, he told me that I had to move it to Wilmington this morning. He told me he was sorry, and that he should have called me.

This new John, the one that doesn't take crap, demanded to know why. Bo told me that their account executive gave him $250 dollars more that I did for the loan, and he needed the money. He needed it? I just had the worst thing happen to me with the miscarriage and he needed it. I was so mad I could barely speak. To make matters worse, Kelly was walking up to the car. She couldn't see me angry or upset, not at this time, or she would think it was the miscarriage that was bothering me. The only customer who knew about our tragedy just made it worse. I couldn't even blast him the way I wanted to because my wife hates confrontations and she was not in a state of mind to hear any other bad news.

How can you do that to someone you call a friend? How can you do that anyone that just went through the hardship of losing a baby? How can you do this to a business partner period? The worst part of it is had I known he had an offer for the loan, I could have called my boss and we would have worked it out to match the amount of money he made from Wilmington. I have no problem with anyone wanting to make the most amount of money on a transaction at all. Just don't promise me business, pretend to be my friend, and not allow me the ability to fight for it.

Here is the most important lesson learned here. Everything in sales is controlled by greed. Nothing else matters to sales people but how much money they can make or what is in it for them. You may hear the acronym WI-IFM someday. It stands for what's in it for me? That's what matters most. I hate stereotypes in life, but I am hard pressed to find someone who did business with me and never mentioned money or reminded me at some point how much business they had given me. The reminder is simple. It is for the mere fact of calling in the favor at a later date in the form of marketing money, sporting event tickets, or a very nice dinner.

When I was trampled for $250 during one of the most painful weeks of my life, I knew it had to change. I knew then that I didn't have the tough skin to be in business to business sales any longer. There are some sales people that would have told Bo to go f*** himself and gotten over it in twenty minutes. That's what makes some sales people so darn good. If you are about to enter into sales, please remember this forever. The tougher your skin, the more likely you are to succeed. I have seen men and women cry over sales. Hell, I have cried over them myself. I've observed people who constantly achieve their goals. I have never seen them upset. This could be a pattern.

I can't help who I am. When someone tells me they will do something, I take them at their word for it. That is the second point here I want to make. Unless it is your brother or sister, never count on business until it is in the door. I had so many people promise me business each month and never return my phone calls. I would go to my boss and tell him all promised business and than have to go back to him weeks later and say my client won't return my call. I remember one time I met a guy who pulled me into his office and said if you give me and my partner five $500 for a seminar, we will work together for a long time. I asked him if he would guarantee me business. He responded by telling me that the senior partner said I am a small town guy and I stand by my word. Good enough for me I thought. Six years later and the guy still hasn't returned my phone call. I guess small town guys have caught the epidemic sweeping the country. This wasn't their fault; it was mine. Please know your customer. How embarrassing.

Chapter 11

Several months later, I opened up a cake from my wife. It had something written on top of it. I could barely make it out but when I did, it said something that changed my life. It read "I'm pregnant." Well, obviously, we didn't want to run out and start celebrating, but it made me happy. Work was going the same month after month. I could never hit 3.5, but I was at 2.5, which didn't make me happy. Still, it was good to be home each night and we were okay financially.

The months seemed to fly by and Kelly was getting bigger and bigger. Our fear gradually changed to excitement. We began preparations with caution, but this time Kelly felt different and our doctor was very reassuring that this baby was doing great inside. Her baby showers came and went. We sold out home and moved to an apartment to get ready to buy a bigger house. We never found out the sex of our child, but Kelly and I were convinced we were having a boy. I recommend to all of you thinking about having your first child not to find out the sex. This is one of the best decisions we ever made .It was like having a huge Christmas gift in front of you for nine months that you wanted to unwrap, but you couldn't. I wanted to name him Bart and have him behave like Bart Simpson.

We went to all of our birthing classes and had a great time during her pregnancy. It is an amazing experience to see a woman transform from one month pregnant to nine months and ready to pop. God really works in amazing ways.

June 26 was a day like any other day. I knew Kelly was close to going into labor, but we both went to work. That afternoon, we met for lunch and Kelly told me she was having contractions. That will certainly make you lose focus on your work day. She told me to go back to work and she would call me. I had read that some women want to be alone right before labor, so I gave her as much as space and time as she needed. Besides, I was having a great month and I wanted to close as many loans as possible. I also wanted to make sure that when I left work to go have our baby, I wouldn't have to think about work until the following week.

At 4:45, Kelly called me.

"I don't think I should be alone anymore," Kelly told me.

I raced home to be with her. We laid together in bed writing down her contraction times in a notebook. It was fun and exciting, but inside I was so tired. I think the mental stress was finally catching up to me, and I caught a brief nap.

Tapping me on the shoulder, Kelly finally told me, "It's time to go to the hospital, John."

It was a ten minute drive, but it felt like a six-hour trip. I was scared and trying desperately to recall all of those things I learned in birthing class. We arrived at the hospital at 10:45 that evening. We called Kelly's doctor, but he wasn't on call, so we got stuck with the one doctor in the practice we didn't want to get. We almost made it through the night without incident until a nurse entered the room at 2:30 a.m. The nurse told us that Kelly needed a medicine for some staph thing she tested positive for. My wife knows her medical records, and she knew she was negative for it. The nurse told her, as per the doctor, that she needed the medicine. We reluctantly agreed.

Thirty minutes after the nurse gave Kelly the medicine, I saw that she looked horrible. Something was desperately wrong. She was red as a lobster and sweating. I immediately went for help. The nurses swarmed the room. Eventually, they got Kelly's temperature down from 102 to 98, but the damage was done. Not only was Kelly correct in that she didn't need the medicine, she was also allergic to it. Our unborn child was now in distress and its heart was beating in the 240 range. For those of you like me who don't know what that means, it was

beating way too fast. We had to make some decisions...
fast.

Kelly and I wanted a natural birth, but time was
against us. The doctor was getting ready to cut Kelly and
take the baby when our two nurses told her to give it one
last try to see if she could push the baby out. Kelly followed everything the nurses told her to do, moving the
baby from one side to another.

Delivery time was near.

She was as brave as anyone could be. I love her for
doing so much. The doctor was nowhere to be found,
which was par for the course as Kelly began to bring Bart
into the world. Kelly worked so hard and pushed like a
champ. When the baby finally arrived, there were more
specialists in the room than I could count. It seemed like
there were six people around the baby and three around
Kelly.

When the baby was ready, they held it up in front
of Kelly and said well what is it? The cord was around
the baby's neck, so when they untangled it, the cord had
fallen in between its legs.

Kelly still groggy and so tired said, "it is a boy."

I began text messaging my family to tell them they
had a nephew and his name would be Ryan. Kelly never
liked the name Bart.

What seemed like hours later, but was only a minute
later, a nurse popped her head up and said "are you sure
it is a boy"?

What?

The boy I had just announced was a myth. I had a girl, and I didn't know what to do with that new information. But I did know this nurse just took my boy - oops girl - out of the room and they were moving real fast. What's wrong with my baby?

Guys, let me give you some first time fatherly advice. When you go to baby classes, you learn how to breathe with your wife, how to change a diaper, how to breathe into a baby doll's mouth, and perform CPR. What they you don't teach you is the thing I had to find out for myself. When your baby comes into the world, check on your wife before you go to see your baby. You and your wife can go see the baby together. It took me a while, but I did it get it right.

After I saw my wife and she looked beautiful, I asked her if I could go see the baby. She said yes, but I could tell she was scared. We saw the way the nurses ran with our baby out of the room. In fact, they never told us where they were taking her.

I went outside and yelled "where are you taking her?"

That's when I heard the words intensive care unit. I watch TV and I know that is the part of the hospital where people who need the most help end up. What's wrong with my baby? I went to the NIC ICU and barged my way into the room. If you are ever feeling sorry for yourself or think that life is so hard, I dare you to go visit a NIC ICU. It is the worst room I have ever been in my life. There were babies with tubes coming out of everywhere. I saw babies so tiny, so defenseless, I couldn't believe it.

The only question I had now was where is my baby?

A nurse approached me and said, " come with me, sir."

"You mean me, I asked her."

"Yes," she replied. "I know your baby, and she looks just like you."

Slowly I walked over to our baby. I was scared, so scared. I had planned for Bart the bad boy. I had a boy who was going to be a soccer star. He was going to be athletic. I approached the incubator and there she was. The little hat, the diaper that wouldn't stay on her legs because they were so skinny. She had that look of what's going on here.

"Can I touch her," I asked the nurse as I peeked into the incubator.

I was afraid I was going to break her. The nurse said yes, so I stuck my hand in there. Now I said earlier how sick the kids were when I walked in the room. My baby wasn't much better. She had things all over her chest and some tubes were in her nose. I gently touched my girl and felt something that I hope everyone feels at least once in their life. My 20-minute old girl touched my hand. It was probably only in my mind, but I am certain she squeezed it.

Bart who?

At that moment in life, I never felt so much love. It overwhelmed me. I adored this little girl and I barely knew her. At nights when Kelly was pregnant, I spoke to Bart in the womb. This little girl was ignored for nine months, and that will never happen again. The way she touched my hand made me cry like a baby. I stood over her for forty-five minutes, just starring into those eyes. She was my girl and now she needed me. I hope she always needs me and I will always be there for her.

While I was watching over this little gift from God, doctors were working on Katie with all sorts of instruments. I knew things weren't okay as a nurse took me by the arm and escorted me away from her. It's funny. You go through life feeling as though you control every aspect of your life, that is until you have a moment like I had in which I had no control. All I wanted was my little girl to be healthy and to share her with my wife.

At this moment I was praying to God to please help us and make sure my little girl recovers from the awful delivery she endured. As I was praying and trying to remain as strong as I could, I heard the words I was dying to hear.

"Are you ready to get your little girl delivered to your room?" a kind doctor asked me.

Oh my God, my girl was going to be okay. I could finally exhale now.

"It was a rough beginning" the doctor told me, "but she is good as new".

I wanted to celebrate or jump in the air. But as I looked around at some of the other babies near me, my better judgment prevailed. Please get me my child and please God look over all these other little angels around me. They need you.

Now our lives finally begin. I can begin preparing to get my girls home and out of this hospital. I finally returned to Kelly and told her our daughter; no name yet, would be joining us shortly. She was healthy and she would be fine. I didn't know it until a few weeks later, but they had to resuscitate her twice in the NIC ICU. She had swallowed so much meconium during her awful labor they had to suction her several times, and the cord around her neck didn't help her breathing either. They finally brought her in and we enjoyed her together. We finally felt like it would be okay to call some family members and tell them our news.

When I turned my phone on, I had eight messages. I knew that none of them would be work calls since I had friends covering my accounts and everyone knew I was at the hospital. Did I say I wouldn't receive work calls? Wrong. Of my eight calls, five of them were family and friends. The other three - you guessed it - work calls and from the same person. Remember earlier that I said the end of the month was the most stressful because you had to get your loans closed?

The baby was born on the 27th; now it is the 28th. June ends on the 30th. We were at the end of the month and Mario, one of loan officers, didn't care that I was at the hospital. In fact, I think it is safe to say that he wouldn't have cared if I were at the hospital for any reason. He feared my account manager, Julie, wasn't giving him enough yield spread, commission for those at home, and he wasn't happy. Once again, I repeat to you sales people. Your customers don't care about you or your family. He had to get paid and he would call my cell phone until he reached me.

My boss took care of the problem, and he was kind enough to come by the hospital and see my daughter. We finally settled on Katherine Ann Cunningham. We call her Katie. Many people asked Kelly and me if we considered legal action due to the incompetence of our doctor. We briefly considered it, but that isn't our style. The last we heard, the entire delivery was under review by the North Carolina Medical Board. As long as this doesn't happen to another couple, we feel as though we did our job.

It wasn't until our regular doctor came in for a visit that we realized how lucky we truly were. The look of anger on his face when he read Kelly's chart told me all I needed to know. Kelly was given the wrong medicine, and it was against our better judgment. Katie had to be resuscitated twice after delivery and she had to have her throat suctioned five times to remove all of the waste she swallowed during labor. She weighed 6.2 pounds at birth but, after all that, she dropped to 5.6. It didn't matter what she weighed or how she looked. We wanted her in the room with us and at home as soon as possible. To all the nurses at CMC Pineville, I say thank you from Kelly and I from the bottom of our hearts. They truly took the time to care for my wife and my daughter. If it weren't for them, we could have had a tragic story to tell.

Chapter 12

We all came home on June 29th. We finally found our house a few months later, and things were going well. I hated when Kelly had to return to work. I loved having them both at home, and my goal one day is to have that.

As for the mortgage industry, it slowly started changing in 2007. Loans were harder to get approved and Wall Street started to push back loans to lenders instead buying them. HSBC was one of the first companies that started to make dramatic changes to their guidelines and rules for lending. Since my territory was one of the poorest, I had to make a decision in 2007 that I hated to make. I had to leave HSBC and move to Washington Mutual. For the next few months I survived at Washington Mutual, but eventually I knew that whole mortgage industry would dissolve.

I stayed in touch with my former coworkers and in the spring of 2007, I received a phone call on a Saturday that devastated me. A former coworker of mine had been killed in a traffic accident. What made matters worse is that his dad worked with us and he was and will always be a dear friend of mine. The young man, Austin Ring, was in his early twenties and just hitting his stride in life. Austin was a wonderful person and a hard working young man, leaving his little brother's baseball game when he was killed in a traffic accident.

I remember being so sad the whole weekend. His dad, Tim, and I were close. Each morning, the two of us would discuss sports and local news, but he always had a way of mentioning one, if not both, of his sons in a conversation. Since I was a new dad during most of these stories, I enjoyed them and thought isn't fatherhood amazing. I had to bring myself to attend the viewing. Because I was with a new company, it would be impossible to attend the day time funeral on Tuesday. I decided I would attend the viewing on Monday evening. All day Monday I found myself to be very nervous. I knew I wanted to go and support Tim, his wife Lori, and son Landon, but I didn't know what to say or how to say it. The words I'm sorry just weren't nearly strong enough.

Tim was burying his son, and I hated for that to happen to him, his family, and friends. I arrived at the church at 7:00. The line wrapped around the entire church. I knew Austin was popular, but the line was truly amazing. As I waited in line, I kept rehearsing what I was going to say. The words I'm sorry and if you need anything kept popping into my head. They just didn't seem strong enough. I wanted to say I love you and give him a bear hug, but that just seemed a little awkward to me. After waiting nearly an hour, I was within five feet of Tim. He looked like he was holding up so strong, but I knew from working with him for two years that he must have been crushed inside. He was burying his son and one of his best friends.

I finally walked up to him and, as I was about to tell him I was sorry, he grabbed me and held me tight. Then he said the words I never expected to hear that evening.

Tim looked at me and said "How's little Katie?"

How's Katie?

Are you kidding me?

I hadn't even thought of her in the last two hours. She was home with mommy. This is the worst evening of Tim's life and here he was asking me about my daughter. I know I spoke about her quite often at work, but this moment is about Tim and his loss. After I heard the words "How's Katie?," I don't remember much of anything else. I can honestly say I don't remember saying goodbye to Tim or any of our conversation past that moment. I just lost it and cried so hard I almost fell into one of my former coworker's arms. Sorry Pedro Rivera.

I still think about that moment. I think about how strong Tim Ring was and will always be. I think there was some divine intervention reminding me to treasure my daughter all of my days because you never know what life has in store for any of us. Tim taught me more that evening about fatherhood than all the books I read combined. If I ever took Katie for granted prior to this evening, it will never happen again. I can't say that anything good came of Austin's death, but I can tell you that it made me realize I wanted to be more like Tim Ring and love my children all of their days. You just never know what is around the corner. I do know this. I hugged Katie tighter after that and watch her even more closely than I did prior to Austin's accident. I can't imagine having to bury a child.

I still speak to Tim on a regular basis. He is one of the strongest people I have ever had the pleasure of knowing. He will do so well in his new venture at State Farm because he is a winner and a role model to anyone who needs to overcome a tragedy. Rest in peace Austin. You will always be missed.

Chapter 13

After the funeral, I was a changed person. I realized that my job was going nowhere and I was tired of waking up nervous. I just watched a friend bury his son and I was starting to realize just how short life was, and I knew I needed a major change. I started looking at monster.com and all the regular sites, but the economy was being affected by the credit crunch and jobs were scarce.

I was slightly distracted in a good way Easter weekend with a visit from my brother. It was great to see Tim, and it was a pleasure to watch him play with his niece. We had a great time the entire weekend. I had to take Tim to the airport the Monday after Easter. As soon as we said goodbye, it all started to hit me. I love my wife and my family, but I hate my career. As I was thinking about all of this, my cell phone started ringing. Who could be bothering me at this early hour? It wasn't 8:00 a.m. yet.

The call was from David Schroeder. He was now with a company named Quint. They are an event and rewards company. They are partnered with the NFL on location, and they can send corporate clients anywhere in the world to any sporting event or entertainment venue. The items are priced relatively high compared to other events, but we are talking about the Super Bowl, Masters, and the Kentucky Derby. Quint has the ability to create an event that people will never forget for the rest of their lives. David and the former head of Decision One, J.C. Faulkner, were partners in this new venture. David offered me a sales executive position. This was the chance I needed, but I knew if I took it I had to go after it hard. There was a huge upside and, with all the people out of work I had to pounce on this job because so many people are unemployed due to the mortgage industry collapse.

The first few months have been rough. I have to cold call fortune 500 companies and get them to spend lots of money with my company in a very tough economy. Along the way I have had to make lots of sacrifices financially and have had moments of stress I wouldn't wish on anyone. I continue to read the paper and see how bad this mortgage collapse is affecting people. There are so many good people out of work it sickens me. The worst part of it all is that people that were in the mortgage business seem to have some negative stigma to them because the word lending or mortgage is on their resume. I worked with some of the brightest people in the mortgage industry and now they can't even get an interview. Meanwhile, the people who made all the wrong decisions are off enjoying their golden parachutes. I hope the people who made money off of the mortgage industry get it together and start hiring some of these folks.

I know that the mortgage industry bought tons of paper, office supplies, and technology devices from national chains while the going was good. Maybe some of these chains can and should return a favor now and hire some people from the mortgage industry. I wish as a society we helped each other more during rough periods. I think we do a great job with national tragedies, but I think during the rough patches we turn a blind eye and say thank goodness it isn't me. Hiring managers reading this book, please don't overlook a resume today that has the keyword mortgage on it. You could be missing out on hiring a person like Ken Luckadoo or P.T. Harbin, who would be an asset to your company.

I hope that the people who worked at Enron or Global Crossing didn't have such a difficult time finding a new job. It's not fair. I get four to five calls a week from people asking for my help to find a job. I want to help everyone through their darkest days, but I can't. Katie and Kelly need me, and I have to get Kelly home out of her job as an assistant superintendent as soon as possible. I dream of the day when I come home from work and there is mommy and daughter waiting for me with the delicious smell of a hot cooked meal in the background. That's my goal for 2008-2009. How do I accomplish this?

Chapter 14

Has anyone written down their goals in the last six months? If you don't write them down and visit them every so often, I feel like you are making a mistake. Put your goals where only you can see them. Hide them and visit them monthly or quarterly. I feel goals should be for you, both personally and professionally. It makes me laugh when I hear people speak about New Year's resolutions. When January comes around each year, my wife and I wait for the people to come in herds to the YMCA to lose their weight and work on that New Year's resolutions. The fitness lines are longer and parking is a mess. By the time February comes, it is shorter lines and business as usual. Why is this? I believe people don't revisit their goals and check progress. Goals should be realistic. If you want to lose 40 pounds, break it up by week. You won't go from 240 to 200 in a week, but you may go to 235.

I think people with reasonable goals are so smart. I wish I had more goals and maybe now that I have accomplished a major goal in writing this book, I can shoot for more. When I was wholesaling annuities in 2000, I weighed 242 pounds. As I said earlier I am 5'10 with dress shoes on. You do the math. My body fat was gross. The way I lost the weight was staying true to a diet and a workout routine. I didn't fast or work out like a madman for six weeks. I found food that was healthy that I enjoyed and workouts I really looked forward to doing. If you hate running, then play sports that will raise your cardio each day. It is the same thing with your job. If you hate your job, how efficiently will you do it?

I remember back in 1999 a Vice President at prudential by the name of Marc Rappaport gave a presentation to a group of us. Marc is a super salesperson and very smart. His entire topic was about joining the misery club. As Marc said, if you join the misery club, you are exiting the promotion club. By that, he meant you will never get promoted or achieve the next level if you are part of the misery club. We all know people in the misery club. They are the people who backstab other workers, run for the elevator at 5:00, and constantly complain. I could never really understand the misery club, even when I first began working and was very impressionable. If you hate something that much, walk away. I always say to my friends that if I were a CEO of a large company, I would require my managers to judge people on the two A's: attitude and ability.

If you have all the ability in the world, but you are mean to people and you aren't a team player, I wouldn't want you on my staff. I think attitude goes a long way. I can remember in the mortgage industry being afraid to call certain underwriters because they were so mean. Yes, they knew their material well and could write loans effectively, but were they really a benefit to the company when sales people refused to speak to them? I am not that naïve to think that all day people should walk around smiling and it is one big party, but I feel any good company is run as a team, and on a team you can't have bad attitudes. How many World Series rings did Barry Bonds win? I rest my case.

I think my hardest chore early in my career was trying to avoid the misery club, but not having them hate me either. People can be vindictive, especially if they see a co-worker on the fast track and they aren't. Avoid the misery club at all costs. As I say until this day, use the four T's in any workplace situation you don't feel comfortable. Take time to think. People who are part of the misery club will wait for you to say one thing wrong, especially gossip, and run with it. I learned that the hard way several times early in my career and it hurt me. I think I was respected at HSBC and Washington Mutual because my superiors could come to me and tell me things they knew wouldn't appear on the internet in five minutes.

If in doubt, always keep your mouth shut. Nothing

good ever comes of gossip. As I said earlier, I hated not being able to say to my boss, Ira you are going to get fired so stop working now. What if by one small chance he took that and ran to human resources? I would have been unemployed as well. It is so hard when you want to protect friends at work, but be certain to protect yourself first. Keeping your mouth closed and your ears open is a great start.

I had one of the worst misery club experiences ever at Prudential. There were seven or eight guys on my team who were just miserable. They hated their jobs, their boss; in fact I think they hated each other. They all wanted to get promoted to wholesaler, but it was very hard. I was so lucky that I was promoted first. From the time it was announced that I was promoted until I left the department, it felt like a life sentence at the hardest prison in the world. I can remember glares and stares when I walked down the hallway. I hated going to work. In fact, I considered using all my vacation time. I was about to make three times, maybe more, the salary of everyone of them. Here is the funny part. Every one of them had been there longer, had more experience, and probably was smarter than me. They all had the worst attitudes in the world and everyone knew it.

I had a plan and I executed it. I heard an interesting quote one time that has stayed with me for a long time: "No one plans to fail, most fail to plan." Take the time to think prior to doing anything in the workplace. The correct answer will usually come to you. If in doubt, call someone who has more experience or someone you trust and respect. I respect David Schroeder a great deal because when you go to him with an idea or a dilemma, he thinks about it and lets you know his thoughts. He doesn't run to the phone to call someone or tell a million people. It is a private conversation and at the end it is handled properly.

Always remember to think before you act. When you get up in the morning before you enter your office or an office of a customer, think about what you want to do and how you will do it. A big mistake I made was trashing my competition or in some cases a coworker to get ahead or win business. Please rise above this. You can be great at your job and never offend anyone else. I used to make fun of companies who had a limited product or no budget to entertain clients. That was wrong. You should discuss your company, your product, your ability. Case closed. Those people out there trashing competitors will get their just due in the end. It happens. It happened to me.

I made some derogatory comments about coworkers over the years. I regret this and will always regret this. I basically told bosses that people weren't doing their job or worse. By doing this, I was jeopardizing people's futures and their family's needs. I am truly sorry for doing this and I won't make that mistake again. The misery club is not exclusive to the workplace. I take Marc Rappaport's comments with me in my every day life.

How many people do you know right now that are

just miserable period? I was at a party the other night when someone was telling me about their boss and how wealthy he was. He then added that he'd never be that rich so he just liked being around him. How do you know you will not be that rich? This person was in the misery club and chances are he isn't coming out. Marc Rappaport is successful at Alpine Funds and will always be successful because he knows to avoid the misery club and enjoy life. I spoke to him the other day and I felt as though I was talking to Tony Robbins. Even though the stock market is off and sales are down, he was in California making presentations, waiting for the markets to turn and be very successful once again. These are the role models I have been so fortunate to have had in my life. I haven't worked with Marc in eight years, but his guidance stays with me always.

Marc isn't a great salesperson because he avoids the misery club. Marc is a super sales person because he is prepared, well versed, and outworks everyone. I remember hearing some of his employees complain because he used to call them early in the morning or on weekends to share a sales idea. How can you complain about someone who wants you to make more money and is sharing expertise or knowledge with you? People who are in the misery club complain, that's who.

Marc is a great father, husband, and friend. Who has a better life than him? Not only does Marc make his family better, he inspires former coworkers each and every day. I would bet anything that Marc's children will all be successful in life, no matter what career path they choose. How can you not be successful when you have a father figure who has a great attitude and works so hard each and every day to give his family the best? The misery club is a lonely, bitter, nasty place. I know that with today's economy, it is hard to be upbeat and positive. I will stay the course Marc inspired me to stay on that which is the positive club. There are people I have worked with in the past that each and every month said I will kill my goal, and they did.

Step one in the positive club: you must know what you want and how to get it. Thanks Marc. I owe a lot of my success in work and in life to you. I hope the people at Alpine Funds realize how lucky they are to have you as a leader.

Chapter 15

As I said earlier, when I was at Prudential I finally realized what I wanted to do and what position I truly wanted. I went for it full steam ahead. I remember what prompted me to change my focus and begin to go for it. My brothers went on a week-long fishing trip in Florida. When they came back, I asked them why no one had bothered to invite me.

My brother said, "It was real expensive. You know how it is."

I knew exactly how it was. I was considered poor and in a middle tier job, and they didn't want to embarrass me by telling me it was $1,500, which I didn't have. This fueled my fire so badly. I looked in the mirror and said what are you doing? I was going to form a plan to get ahead and execute it. I was so insulted by not being invited to a special event. The sad thing is my brothers were correct and they were trying to protect me. Whether I was right or wrong, I was going to push myself and get noticed until I got promoted, or I would leave the company.

When I played soccer I was a goal keeper. I loved it when people looked at my height and said you can't be very good. Bring it on. You just declared war. I was good and I could be good, no great, in the business world. The first step I took in my plan of attack was my hours of operation. If you aren't in the office before your boss at least twice a week, I feel that is a big mistake. Arrive early. All bosses like it when they arrive and their team is operating bright and early. People who come into work early generally like their job. I still find it amazing when I hear people say they are late for work with no excuse such as traffic. Unemployment is at 5% and you are going to take a chance on getting fired because you can't get to work on time. That is scary.

As I said earlier, be positive, have a great attitude, and keep it that way. Make sure your appearance is top notch. You don't have to be rich to look good. Make sure you always look good. Shine those shoes, look for good bargains on designer shirts, always look your best. Save a special shirt for a special occasion. Business casual has become somewhat casual to me. Take it up a notch. If your boss had an emergency and needed someone to fill in on an important meeting for him, the first thing he or she would do is look to see who looks good today. Be that person. Dress for success.

The next part is simple. The most important part of your job now is to want it. You must want to be in your chair, you must want success, you must want to impress everyone you work for and work with. I wanted it so bad I would take a train to Newark on Saturdays, which isn't the safest place in the country, just to get caught up and work some more. No lies here. I would send out emails, and this was before laptops, to make sure my boss knew I was working on Saturdays. I wanted it so badly I made it a point to tell myself each day to be better than yesterday.

As I said earlier, it is all about attitude and ability. You must have ability. If you aren't sure about something at work, if something limits your production, you must learn it. I had a situation in which I needed to use Excel and do some very tough calculations on it. I hate, hate, hate Excel. I knew I needed it, and in a workforce where people are competitive and competing for the same promotion, you will not get much help. I ended up hiring a tutor who came into my office after hours and worked with me on my computer. I was so afraid not all Excel programs were the same that I insisted we did it on my computer. I hated to do it. I wanted to be home. I didn't want to spend the $500, but it had to be done.

You can't skip steps at work. If you don't know it, make the time to learn it. If you dress for success, if you want it badly, you can achieve it.

The last point I would make on achieving success is this. How many people know you want to get promoted? Does your boss know you want more and you seek a promotion? You must schedule time with your boss at least once a month. I don't care what industry you are in, you must speak one-on-one with your boss behind closed doors. Create a Word document and email it to your boss a few days prior outlining what topics you wish to discuss. It shows your boss you respect their time and that you are organized. Create an appointment and have an agenda. If you ask for monthly appointments and have good open dialogue with your boss, your annual review should be no surprise at all. Most people that are in a bonus pool need to know this. Most times, your annual bonus is tied to your annual review.

Don't take any chances with your review. Get in front of your boss and ask how am I doing? I'm not saying that this is all it takes to be successful or to get ahead but these actions will certainly assist your cause.

Chapter 16

Remember earlier when I said take as many training classes as you can? I took one back in 2003 in Boston. It was the Sequoia training for sales people. The instructor was terrific. I highly recommend this class to anyone who does any type of public speaking. The instructor said something during our training that has stayed with me all of my professional days. He said write down your strengths and weaknesses. They are your weaknesses and you will likely not improve upon them enough to make a difference. That's why you should focus on your strengths. There is a reason I am not an accountant. I hate numbers and always will. I am not strong at math, no matter how many classes I have taken. I don't like it. Why bother trying to perfect something your heart doesn't have time for?

I know my strengths and now I work hard to make them even better every day. My strengths are public speaking, customer service, creative writing, strong follow-up skills, execution of ideas, and a strong team player. These are six strengths in which I feel I can improve and make myself very marketable. My weaknesses are math, computer skills, need tougher skin, and I am not a slick sales person. Being a slick sales person isn't a bad thing. You just have to be very good at being slick and make sure your customer appreciates your style.

Another way to create your list of strengths and weaknesses is to go back and dig out your old employee reviews. If you respect your bosses in the past, go back and read what they had to say about you. If you are just finishing college, look at your transcripts. Which classes did you excel at and why?

Discovering your inner strength just doesn't apply to your professional life. I know when it comes to my daughter, I can't stand to see her in pain. Hence, my wife takes her to any doctor's appointment that requires shots. My wife isn't a mean person at all. She just has a better way of dealing with it. Notice on my strength list there is no mention of being mechanically inclined in any way, shape, or form. I knew when we bought this house that I had to get a home warranty to protect the house in case anything went wrong. It's the best $500 I spend a year.

People today insure many things. You buy life insurance, home insurance, and health insurance for the reason just in case. People never insure their career. The best way to insure your career in the event of a mortgage collapse or an Enron, or lousy executive, is to work your skills and develop your strengths until they are perfections. There weren't many differences between selling annuities and mortgages. The company structures were similar and the concept was the same.

In today's society, you have to be able to cross industries and be able to transition from one job to the next. The way to do that is to make sure your tools are sharpened and you are confident in yourself. I heard a story once that Larry Bird practiced his free throws prior to his last game. Here is a legend that had every reason not to practice, but found the time to do it one last time because he wanted to end his career on a high note. He had millions in the bank, a place in the hall of fame reserved, and championship rings on his fingers, yet he found the time. It is your career. It is your life. Please make the most of it.

There are many books coming out on the topic of inner strength and how to realize one's inner strength. I think a very good way to learn more about your inner strength is to ask people around you who truly care about you what they feel your strengths and weaknesses are. If you can get a coworker or, better yet, a customer to answer those questions, think how much better you could become at your job. I remember one time I asked a customer of mine how he liked my presentation.

He looked at me and said, "Son you speak so fast I

haven't listened to you in months. I'm here for the ribs and hush puppies."

Truth be told he was right. I did speak way too fast and that is something I constantly work on.

Chapter 17

Does anyone know what the greatest fear in America is? It is public speaking. Death was number two. If you can speak in public, you are in select company. I have never minded it. I have spoken in front of groups of close to five hundred people. I think for me it is a natural characteristic. I don't think there is a trick to being a successful public speaker. There are so many people who are wonderful public speakers. John F. Kennedy was brilliant. President Clinton, by the time this book comes out I might have to say President Bill Clinton, is brilliant. If you ever want to see some great public speakers, turn on the USA network on Monday evenings. Watch professional wrestling and you will see what I mean. The Rock, Stone Cold Steve Austin, Triple H, and of course Charlotte's own Ric Flair are sensational. They grab a microphone and speak in front of 20,000 people without a stutter.

I believe when someone delivers a great speech, it is because of two things: preparation and they care. If you care about how your presentation is going to sound to your audience, you will rehearse it, research it, and conquer it. I see Joel Osteen on TV every so often. It doesn't surprise me that he can fill a huge arena with people. That man gives everything he has to his presentation. I'm not sure I have ever listened to his sermon or received the message from it, but I know with the emotion and conviction he speaks impresses me each time I see him. That's all it takes to deliver a good speech.

I have worked with people who were smart, energetic, and were terrible speakers. The reason for this I felt was that they didn't approach a speech as seriously as they should have. Know your target audience. Be respectful of their time and prepare weeks before you address a crowd. One trick I learned was to ask someone prior to presenting a little bit about the audience. Does this group mind a longer presentation? Do they ask tough questions? What bothers this group about presenters? Know your audience. Research your topic and your audience. The great speakers such as Tony Robbins have charm and charisma to add to it, and that's why they are special.

But if you have to deliver a speech, the first thing you must do is research the topic until you are blue in the face. It was amazing to me when I hear coworkers or competitors stand up and give a presentation and they are not be able to answer a question on their product.

How can you stand up and deliver a message when you don't know the topic? Research your topic until you can't read any longer and then do it again. If you care about it, you will deliver it like you never have before. When you think of John F. Kennedy, you think of "ask what you can do for your country." He said it with conviction and he cared.

I once spoke to a group of financial advisors in Florida. I was the last speaker of ten. The advisors were tired and I stood between them and a free round of golf. Remember, sales people love free things. I took my presentation and split it up. I would look at a slide, go over it, and then the next slide I would bypass and say golf. I received more compliments from that presentation than any other presenter.

Know your audience. There are times when your crowd wants information and they need to be educated. While you are giving your presentation, look at your audience and look at body language. If people are fidgeting or moving, they are distracted and possibly bored. Liven it up a little. If people are sitting in front of you and their arms are folded, this means they are defensive and they don't trust what you are saying. Other times, they need someone to amuse them and have a little fun with them. Someone told me something when I first started public speaking that made a lot of sense. People go to church on the weekend for sermons. Don't give a sermon. Give a good, brief, well thought out presentation. Chances are, if you feel like you are going on too long, you are.

A good presentation doesn't have to be long; it has to be effective. Never take a chance by telling a joke that will upset someone due to religion, race, sexuality, or any other way you could offend someone. The best target of a joke is you. I would keep the jokes to a minimum or people lose sight of who you are and what you are selling or presenting to them. Lastly, if you have the technology, videotape yourself before you speak to a crowd. The first time I was taped, I despised it. Be your harshest critic. You will pick up hand gestures, pacing, not making eye contact with the crowd so effectively. I hated hearing and watching myself on tape. Now I don't mind. It also reminds me to get my fat butt to the gym

Chapter 18

I know that in the last five years I have been through a lot. I have traveled all over the country looking for business and trying my best each and every day. I have had some months that I never wanted to end, and I have had months that I couldn't wait to end. I have worked with some great people and there are former coworkers and clients who I have the most respect for. For those of you who stood by and tried to help me, I can't say thank you enough. For those of you who took advantage of me, I just want to say publicly that I forgive you and I harbor no ill will. I don't understand why people would use someone and take advantage of them, but that is life.

I mentioned earlier that I am Catholic and I try each day to become a better Catholic. As we get older, I think some of us feel a need to grow closer to God. That is certainly true in my case. One topic that comes up in church quite often is forgiveness. The priests at St. Matthew preach forgiveness. Forgive thy neighbor. I know it sounds easy, but it may be the hardest thing to do in the world. How does one forgive someone who promises you business and breaks their word? As someone who was on the receiving end of that issue more than once, I know it is so hard to forgive. For me, I just know that I must move on and let it go.

You can practice to avoid being taken advantage of and try to plan ways to avoid it. I have known some sales people who would never give out money, or tickets, or anything until the business had come to them. I applaud them for that, but my question is if you don't spend money, how can you make it? Some people can do just that and I admire them so much for having that ability. Folks, it is similar. A sale is like anything else; it is all trial and error.

You must make great first impressions and work off of that. I read something that said it takes eight good impressions to overcome a bad first impression. I find this to be entirely true. When you start a new position, please remember that. Whether you are a customer service representative, a CEO, or a salesperson, all eyes are on you when you first start your job. Bring a great attitude with you and make sure people want to be around you. Don't try too hard to be everyone's best friend, just try to fit in on the team.

I know that when I walked into an office for the first

time, all I wanted was everyone to like me and I wanted to connect with everyone from the receptionist to the branch manager. I used to look for items on desks such as pictures or diplomas to connect with that person. I went too far with it because people might have remembered that I went to Villanova, but they never remembered that my annuity was good and I needed their business. If you are in sales, when you go on a sales call remember that you are there to educate, gather information, and close deals.

Speaking of gathering information, this was probably one of my biggest weaknesses. Lou Holtz, I believe, once said "God gave you two ears and one mouth so you should speak half the time you listen." This is so true. I have the problem of getting so excited when I meet someone that I want to talk and talk. The only way to find out about someone or their business is to ask questions and truly listen to their answers. You will be amazed how much you learn when you truly listen to someone. When someone asks about you, tell them briefly but, most importantly, tell them how you do business.

Set your expectations as you want your business partner to set theirs. Perhaps you may want to email some of this information just so both parties have it in writing. I don't like bad surprises. Unfortunately, I had a great deal of them while I was in sales. Try to eliminate the surprises as much as you can. Communicate with your customers as often as possible. Let your customers know what is going on at all times. If your product has a change or something bad is about to happen with your company, pick up the phone and call them right away.

I was terrible about having to deliver bad news. I don't think many people are good at it. I just hated the thought of being considered the bad guy. I had a situation once where a financial advisor sold my product incorrectly to his client. He called me and asked me a question to clarify, and I gave them the wrong response. I sat in my car on a 100 degree day for two hours figuring out a way to tell him I was wrong. By the time I called him, he had called my boss ranting and raving, and told my boss he never wanted me in his office again. The whole mess could have been prevented if I had picked up the phone and called him back immediately. That situation would have taken at least 12 good impressions to overcome. I never would have had the time. It was a good office for business, too. That was totally my fault.

Being in sales is like owning a 7-11. All 7-11s look alike, but for the most part they are independent franchises. You should always consider yourself a contractor, but the bottom line is your prized possession You must make more money than you spend, and if someone is taking up too much time at your cash register, politely ask them to step aside. Speaking of which, if you are walking into an office and a customer has a lot of time for you and you sit in their office for a great deal of time and their phone never rings, that probably happens for a reason. They probably don't have a great deal of business going on and will end up being a waste of your time.

The most important possession each day for you is your time. Please use your time wisely. If you feel like every day is Groundhog Day and you are constantly arriving home or to your hotel late at night with nothing to show for it, examine your situation immediately. There is so much time I would like to have back from the last five years. There were so many nights I stayed up worrying about sales numbers or hearing from my boss. I know that I can never get that time back, but I would sure like to.

I remember in 2003 when I was wholesaling annuities for AIG. I was having trouble getting into offices to see potential clients. All the offices were booked up or weren't going to see me. I called a good friend who was a broker in Myrtle Beach. I asked him if I could come in and present to his office. I needed to put something on my calendar for my boss to see and I hated lying about office visits. That darn Catholic guilt thing. My friend told me he would like to see me, but that his office didn't like my product and they weren't doing much annuity business anyway. I said that's okay, I want to do it.

I drove eight hours round trip with traffic, and he was so right. I walked around an office and had the worst conversations. How could I have spent that time better? I could probably think of a million ways. It is five years later and I still think about it, which tells me I really regret making that trip. Time is a commodity, and it is one that you should never take for granted. Now that I have a wife and daughter, my time is now so important.

Chapter 19

One valuable lesson I learned this year came from my brother. He told me to lose the word blame from my vocabulary. It is so easy when the chips are down to blame someone or something for your misfortunes in life. It is so easy now to blame Greenspan or Bush for the economic hardships out there. It is so easy to say the Iraq war has caused fuel prices to soar and my company decided to have cutbacks. These are reasons for bad things happening, but don't use them as excuses. If you are down and out, blame yourself.

There are people all around you doing great and having record years. Quint just sold a bunch of Masters Packages and Kentucky Derby tickets last month. These are some of the highest priced tickets on the market. People paid top dollar and never flinched. This tells me that there are industries doing well and people have money. You just have to know how to find it and how to execute on it.

For those of you who don't read the Wall Street Journal, you are not a business person in my opinion. You must know at all times which industries are doing well and which ones are faltering. You must research the world economy as often as possible. Instead of reading the internet to see which Cincinnati Bengal was arrested last night, you should read educational items that will help your future. Look at companies that have strong earnings. These companies typically aren't downsizing and perhaps they are hiring. A lot of managers will tell you that you must outwork the competition. I believe you must out think them.

Consider your professional life as a continuous chess match. You have to be one step ahead. If you see your industry facing challenging times, you have two choices. The first is to leave as I said earlier, or the second is the one I discovered this year, which is to supplement your income. There is nothing wrong with working multiple jobs or having supplemental income.

My CPA works for a company and he does taxes on the side. He started his side business driving around neighborhoods dropping his business card in mail boxes. He started in 2002 with a 1986 Volvo and he now has a 2007 Lexus. He gets it. He wanted more out of life. He saw his potential with his company and wanted to add to it. He keeps his benefits and a good salary with his employer, and he adds to that bottom line by doing over 100 tax returns and consulting small business owners on the side. Isn't that the American dream? Half of the day he is an employee and the other half he is his own boss. Good for you, Randy.

I began to look for my second career a few months ago. I wrote down a list of things I wanted to do and I broke it down like this.

What am I really good at?

What can I do that I can make money at?

What can I do that would require the least amount of money down, i.e., lowest overhead?

What would I enjoy doing? It is my company and why shouldn't I enjoy it.

What service can I provide to the public that they need?

Will this take me away from my family?

I truly love working with children. Ever since I was a young boy playing sports, I have always admired coaches. I began volunteering at the YMCA four years ago. I have played soccer since I was 6 years old, which means I have thirty-two years experience. I decided to give back and dedicate myself to children, like people such as Ray Cotto did for me back in Hazlet, NJ. I began coaching very small children and now I work with ten-year olds.

The first thing I realized was that kids today are different than when I was a child. Kids today don't have the ability to play like we did when we were younger. I personally don't feel that today's kids are as tough, they aren't in shape, and they don't want it like we did. I think there are many reasons for that. Parents today are mostly dual income families. Kids can't leave their homes and go to parks or fields due to the increase in abductions and crimes, and kids today have more than we ever did, at least more than I did. This makes kids, in my opinion, not as aggressive, not as good, and in worse shape than ever.

I can honestly say that I would be afraid to ask my kids to run a mile. I would say two of my players could run that distance. There is an epidemic going on where some kids are just overweight, perhaps lazy, and not ready to play sports at a recreational level. Now I do know that there are other kids who play highly competitive sports and they are terrific. However, the mass number of kids need help and fast.

I won a special award from the YMCA for coach of the year. The award was due to the talent improvement of my players. If you are going to play for me, you will do it the right way. I am a tough coach with a no nonsense approach.

Several years ago, I was coaching and a player's mother approached me and said "I wish you could come over to our house and yell at him like you do on the field. He responds to you better than his father."

I was flattered at first and then when I thought about it, I became alarmed. I yelled at their son because he wasn't listening and he needed a boot in the ass. Are parents that afraid of yelling at their children they want a stranger to do it? But maybe this woman was telling me something I needed to hear. Kids do respond to me in a good way. The YMCA gave me an award, parents are praising me, and we win games. The answer to question number one is yes I am really good at coaching soccer.

Soccer is a cheap sport to play. You need soccer shoes, a ball, and shin guards. There are fields everywhere, so it isn't like ice hockey where you have to pay a great deal of money to register. That would answer question number two for me. To instruct kids in soccer, I would need a field. The overhead is quite low. If I begin coaching or tutoring on the side, I can make some money. If I become really good at it and perfect it as a business, I can make a great deal of money with virtually no overhead. Consider this. When my wife and I go out to dinner, we pay a babysitter $9 an hour. She comes over and watches our baby sleep. Her sole purpose is to be at the house in case of an emergency. What is my value if I work with children? I am providing the family with babysitting, teaching, mentoring, and most importantly coaching them to be better in life. My value is at least $20 an hour if not more.

The answer to number three is yes, I would enjoy it. I volunteer because I like it, so opening up my own soccer school or coaching clinic would be something I know I would like.

The answer to number four is simple. I would provide parents a place to take their kids where they will become better athletes and better soccer players. Instead of taking your children to the movies or to the mall, take them to me. We will play hard, have some laughs, and gain confidence for high school, which is right around the corner. Have you ever seen a karate studio on a Saturday? They are always packed. Parents want their kids out of the house. Please bring them to my field. I can do this on my schedule, so the answer to number five is yes. I can still spend time with my family and schedule training sessions at my leisure.

I am five for five in questions. The Cunningham Soccer School will be open soon. The best part about this whole thing is the things I will never have to do again. I will never have to fill out a call report or an activity sheet. I never minded doing them, but they were always a reminder that you worked for someone else and they could have you complete work any time they wanted you to. Now I will fill out cards - Hallmark cards telling people like my mother, my wife, and my daughter how much I love them. It sounds quite corny doesn't it? Good, because I can't wait to do it.

The freedom I am developing allows me to open up my mind and my heart to help others along the way. I am free from conference calls, meetings, and events that took me away from my daughter. Last week, I spoke to a man who wanted to fly him and his wife to the Kentucky Derby. He wanted first class seats and he wanted a butler in his suite. He also wanted a private room so his wife wouldn't feel smothered. I asked him if he does these types of events quite often. His response to me was I love my wife I will do anything for her. He told me that they don't own a TV any longer. He said when people ask him what they do now without a TV, he said we make out. That's what I want. David Smith, thank you for helping me realize what I want.

I know that before I begin taking money, I will visit Randy, my CPA, and get business advice. I don't want the IRS chasing me. I feel everyone should see a CPA. Just ask Wesley Snipes. But most importantly, I want to ask Randy if he knows he inspired me to follow him and make my own way. As my brother Tom, said earlier, don't blame anyone, just get it done.

Most of you have heard the word networking. I hear people say I have to network and then they join a public speaking group, or they join a young professional association. Networking is what you do every day. Networking to me is utilizing your social skills in any way you can. I have met so many people though volunteering, being sociable at a coffee house, or saying hello to someone at the gym. I am not saying professional associations are bad at all. They can be fun and can lead to long lasting benefits. What I am saying is remember that if you go to networking meetings, you will be surrounded by people who are all in the same boat and are all looking for jobs or business.

Branch out and do different things or activities where you can meet people who aren't looking for anything. For example, I coached a child whose father was the CEO of a very large food company. He never would have attended social meetings or networking events. I met him and have done business with him because I provided a service to his family. If you are new to a city, get off of your butt and get involved. Volunteer, join sports clubs, or join a book club. Just become part of the community. That is where you will meet people who can help your career and you personally.

You may be able to help some people, too. Make sure people know what you do for a living. People can be so good natured. If they know you work for a bank and they see on the news the bank has layoffs, they may reach out for you without you even knowing it. They may make phone calls on your behalf. That's what you want. You want people who will look out for you. I have a family member who became unemployed and he was unemployed for six days because a friend heard about it and hired him. That was back in 1999, and he is still with that employer. If you aren't sociable by nature ,try to find friends that are. They can help you get into clubs or organizations.

Charlotte is a great city for networking, but no one will come to your front door and ask you to join. You must make the effort. I have four friends that were former professional football players. I met them at a meeting I went to by mistake, but now we all look out for each other and have strong bonds. Tomorrow, I am going to lunch with the former heavyweight champion Calvin Brock. We met at a small business association meeting and now we speak regularly. It isn't just idle chatter. We pick each other's brains on ventures and we both want to succeed in our next careers.

Networking has opened doors for me that were once closed. I know that I can pick up the phone this evening and call four former NFL players if I wanted to. How many people who have never played a professional sport or are an agent can say that? It isn't bragging on my part. It is the fruit of networking. Get involved. Do something tomorrow evening you have never done before. As I said earlier, your time is valuable so use it wisely.

Networking is a valuable tool for so many reasons. You may learn about other companies in your city that you never knew existed. Someone may help you in other ways outside of the business arena. I truly enjoy networking now more than I ever had, and my business life is strong. Now I want to network to meet others and perhaps meet someone who is in need of assistance. I met my wife because two mutual friends set us up. There is no stronger testament to networking than that, no Kelly, no Katie.

Chapter 20

I keep waiting for my break like I did in 1998, 1999, and 2000. I know my breaks are coming and I am proud to say I sold $60,000 worth of Kentucky Derby packages. But this time it is different. I won't wait for anything. I will make my break. The reason I bring up selling $60,000 worth of packages is so important to me. It means I can sell and I can cross over from one industry to the next and sell. The commission on this sale will be average, not great. The commission earned means more to me than anything in my professional life right now. It means I can do it and I did it. I never changed my approach and I went after it. After all the months of hardship and self doubt, I achieved something. I didn't hit it big enough to buy a new car or plan a dream vacation, but I did achieve the beginning of getting my self-esteem back. Sometimes that is more important than a big paycheck.

I sold something to a customer who had choices. They chose me and it feels right. It almost makes me feel like I did in 1998 when sales were so easy to come by. A good month will help me to erase some of the doubt in myself and my abilities. I have had so many bosses in the past help to create inner doubt. This month is dedicated to all of you who told me I didn't have it. I have some major clients coming on board, but still the harder days will out number the good days. Through it all, I have had some thoughts about throwing in the towel or giving up. I have doubted myself more the last two years than in my whole life.

Looking back at it now, I feel doubt is great. I think self-doubt made me mad and made me change my way of thinking. I used to think how many rejections will I have today or how bad can today be. The difference between doubt and success is your belief. You must believe you are going to win. The New York Giants were doubted by everyone in the Super Bowl. I think I saw one so called expert predict they would win one out of a hundred games. The Giants used this to their advantage and went out and won it all.

Let other people doubt you and show them what you can do. You must believe in what you are doing. If you don't believe you are going to win, you will lose. That isn't a sports analogy; it is a life lesson. I have wanted to quit and tell my wife I can't do this. The thing that stops me is this little package that follows me around and says Daddy. I can't stop thinking about her and I have to provide for her. She needs her Daddy, so I can't quit and run away. I can only remember the hand squeezing my hand in the hospital. It has almost been two years, but I still remember it like it was yesterday. I have some great other things in the hopper for side business and I have to act on them.

The other lesson I learned was to align yourself with people who are positive and also believe in you. The person I have known the longest in Charlotte is Joel Glasco. We have been friends for eight years. Anytime I have self doubts or am considering a career change, I look to Joel for advice. He believes in me and cares about my best interests. There is a reason Joel is so successful at Wachovia Securities. He is a great listener and a tremendous leader. I look up to Joel because he has blazed a career path one would be proud of. I thank Joel for his friendship and guidance.

Who says you can only have two jobs? Every time I look at someone like Sean Combs, I am in total awe. He started as a rapper and now it is easier to count the ventures he isn't involved with. In fact, from Katie I learned something that translates to business. I learned the word love. Love your daughter and more importantly love your life. If I can get so much happiness from her, why can't I get it from my job? The answer is in front of all of us and I think we ignore it. What do we love to do? I can mix my two businesses together, never have to travel again, and make a great living. I have found my inner talent and strength, and it was due to a baby. Instead of worrying about numbers, volume, travel, and dying an early death, I will create the best soccer camps and teach each child with the love I have for my daughter.

I encourage everyone to find something to do that you love. I know it sounds corny, but I get excited thinking about it. While you are the person at the water cooler gossiping about whether you will lose your job, I will be on the field playing keep-away with my kids. I want to do something that gives me personal gain, but also something no one can take away from me. This isn't America in the 1950s, where everyone worked for one company until they got their watch and their pension and bought a rocking chair. I think the last time I looked, the average American will work for five companies during their career on average. I don't want that.

While I am coaching my kids, developing talent, and meeting parents, I don't have to worry about the stock market, the gas prices, and the election. I can change my prices to reflect what's going on to help parents, but I won't be downsized. How can one downsize them self? I ask everyone to find that one thing you are so good at and perfect it. If you are downsized or if you meet a boss like I had in the past, you will be okay. With the support of the folks at Quintevents and my passion to instruct children, I can't miss. It took a baby coming into the world to teach me that there is so much more to life than numbers. The number that matters is one. One dream, one major goal, but most importantly you have one life. Live it well. I can be down, out, broke, hurting, but as long as each morning I hear the pitter patter and the scream Daddiieeeeee, I am wealthy, healthy, and successful.

Now I must work on my health. I mentioned appearance earlier. Appearance is important for two reasons. The first reason is because so many people judge you by how you look. Each day, everyone should find thirty minutes to at least to go for a walk, ride a bike, or throw around some weights. I know when I weigh less than 180 pounds, I feel better and I work better. Try to get out during a stressful day and hit the gym. Sales people, coworkers, management - they all notice appearance. If a salesperson is considering bringing you to a meeting with an important client, your looks certainly matter. Hiring managers will never tell you that you are too heavy for the job, but they will find another reason not to hire you.

Many companies today avoid hiring the unhealthy due to increasing health insurance costs. You will never find this in an employment guide, but I assure you it happens every day. Wal-Mart is contesting paying a woman's $200,000 medical claim. If Wal-Mart is cost conscious, imagine what smaller companies are trying to avoid. A bad appearance, particularly being overweight, can cause a manager to consider you lazy. It also can be a sign of someone about to develop diabetes or have a heart attack.

I have had many managers make comments about

my weight. It hurts when someone says something about your weight. My managers were awful for saying that, but I knew exactly what they meant. Get it together. We don't want people out representing us that look bad. There is a reason the company logo is in much bigger and bolder print than your name on your business card. Think back to when you met your spouse. You were immediately attracted to his or her looks well before their intelligence, personality, and sense of humor. I said earlier how important a first impression is to people. The first impression anyone has is your looks.

The second reason you need to work on yourself is simple. You want to be around for a long time. Now that I have Kelly and Katie, I want to be around for them for a long time. I hate the fact that my father won't have the chance to hold Katie. I also hate that my Aunt Dorothy won't be able to sit with my mother and watch Katie tear apart her house. They both died from overworking and, in my medical opinion, stress. My father went to the dentist regularly to make sure he looked good. However, he never went to a doctor for a check up. His theory was that coworkers and friends can't see my clogged arteries or my high blood pressure, but they can certainly see brown teeth.

Your company enrolls you in medical plans and charges you each paycheck. Suck it up, pay the co-pay, and get yourself checked. One of my favorite college basketball coaches, Skip Prosser, died in his office in his mid fifties. I am not sure he could have seen a cardiologist and prevented his heart attack, but I wish that he had. Instead, he was probably recruiting players, working on new plays, and focused on winning. It is a sign of the times. We just don't pay attention to the little things. I am not knocking Skip Prosser at all. I wish he were still around coaching Wake Forest.

Ask your doctor whether you should be taking an aspirin or fish oil each morning. So what if you have fish breath at six in the morning. You will be healthy. With all the stress so many Americans have been under the last few years, we should have a national holiday called go get yourself checked day. Everyone is invited, except the big oil company executives. Please stay at work. You deserve it. I'm kidding. You guys come, too. Just stay at the end of the line. See, I already stopped blaming people for our troubles and I forgive them for high gas prices, and it feels good.

In the last four years, I have had heart problems, kidney stones, and ulcer symptoms. I am thirty-nine years old for crying out loud. I need to watch my diet, exercise, and find time to visit doctors. I no longer have a choice. I am living for three, and who knows maybe four. Bart is still out there and a possibility. This is all a realization because of a beautiful woman named Kelly Cunningham and a girl named Katie. Five years ago, my life was work, buffalo wings, and beer. Now, my life is smart work habits, spending time with my girls, and volunteering as much as I can. I will take that trade any day of the week.

I no longer know what a hangover is. I can't tell you the last time I closed a bar. I can tell you the last time I woke up to a little girl having a nightmare and holding her until she gently falls back to sleep. That was last week. I hate to admit it, but I love when she has nightmares. She holds on to me so tight. Life has changed for me forever.

When I get the so-called hall pass, I still enjoy it with my friends John Scott and Kevin O'Herron. The nights are still enjoyable, just so different. Instead of going out to a bar and looking for a woman, I avoid women and we discuss important topics such as 529 plans for Katie or a get away weekend with Kelly. When I think about the past, I become very proud of myself. I did stupid things and had some fun. I have learned from most of my mistakes and pray to God history will never repeat itself. I don't want to change anything from my past. I just want to leave it there.

It is Friday evening and my girls are asleep. I can go anywhere and do anything, but I'm just where I want to be. I am writing about them and keeping them safe. I might go in and peek in on Katie. I love it when she sleeps with that little butt in the air. Some of you may say I am getting old. I say I am getting smarter and my heart is growing each day. I know it is impossible for your heart to grow bigger, but my heart grows fonder each day. It grows for my girls. I can't make them proud if I am not around. Maybe I should write that down as one of my new goals. I want to live until I am in my eighties. If that's the case, maybe I should go on the 5k run tomorrow with Kelly. No, sorry I can't. I have ten soccer players who will win their first game tomorrow. We have lost four in a row and we are due for a victory. It doesn't matter if we win or lose. They will play hard and make me proud. They'd better, darn it, or laps will be run at practice on Tuesday.

Chapter 21

I keep saying I have two girls in my life, but I actually have five. I haven't seen my wonderful mother in almost a year. She lives in New Jersey and I need to get up there soon. While I am there, I will also see my sister Annmarie. I miss you too, baby. She is also a Villanova graduate and is the reason I went there. She is bright and successful. She is also one of the first people to see my book. First signed book is for you Annie Potts.

We have so much fun when we are together and once again it is has been too long. My mother in law is the mother in law every guy wants. She is fun, so sweet, and never meddles. Thanks for being you, Elouise McCarthy. And last of all, my sister in law Julie. She is fun, smart, and great to hang out around with and someone who impresses me each day. If she weren't being a mother to my two beautiful nieces, Emily Sullivan and Anna Sullivan, she should write a book. She is the writer in the family.

I also have four brothers who I am so proud to call my brothers. Tom, you are a role model to me. Your kindness, intelligence, and personality are so special. You have helped me so many times when I didn't think anyone cared. Tim, you are a great guy and I love when you come to visit. It has been too long. Please come down soon because we all miss you. Make sure you bring your new bride Trina. We need to get to know her better. Katie misses her uncle Brian very much. She asks for you all the time as we all do. Kenny, you are the youngest of all us, but your wisdom, determination, and the way you handle yourself impress me every day. As far as I am concerned, you won the Wall Street boxing tournament just by getting in the ring. Way to go champ. Kenny Sullivan, you are not a brother in law, you are my brother. I can't think of someone I would rather have as a brother in law than you. I hate that you live three hours away. You would be the fourth out with us on the weekends at the bar.

I mentioned earlier that I lost my father when I was thirty two. I miss him and wish he were around. I always tried to impress him and win his affection. Well, I now have a new person to try to impress. Mickey McCarthy, I am proud to call you father in law. You have been such a tremendous person to be around. You are not a father in law, you are a dear friend. We talk for hours and we always have a great time. If I could ever get you to eat healthier, you would be perfect. Thanks for being you. Mickey and

Elouise, thanks for having a wonderful daughter. Both of you should take a bow. You raised two great girls. You are wonderful grandparents and I know Katie misses you so much. We all miss you.

I'm so happy today is Friday. I used to hate weekends because I couldn't get business. I actually had a coworker tell me one time that he hated the weekends because work was his life. He has two daughters. Gannon, I hope you take time away and realize your girls will grow up so fast. Katie is now talking and walking, and I don't want to miss a thing. Weekends are now perfect. They give me time away from the office and time to play with my girls. Sunday mornings are my favorite. When we all go to church, it just feels so right. I pray for so many things such as my family, good health for everyone, and the war to end. I look to my right and I know that my prayers were answered because there are my girls.

Chapter 22

Last night I heard something that broke my heart and it made me stop and think. A friend of ours told us that she knew someone who took his own life due to financial problems. He owned a company and, like so many, was suffering due to the economy. This man left behind a family. These are some of the worst times ever. I wouldn't compare it to the depression, but it is worse than anything I have ever seen. Please remember that bull markets always come after bear markets. Nothing is so bad that you take your own life. The suffering you end will only cause so much more for those who love you. Fight through this bump in the road. If you've accumulated a ton of debt, just remember this. Your government will have that times several trillion.

So many people fall on hard times and make it back.

Thanks, Roy. You are a champion and oh so right. Donald Trump, who I admire so much, had his bump in the road and look at him now. Donald Trump recently conducted a celebrity apprentice. He had some very high profile celebrities trying to win money for their charity. Every one of the celebrities on the show addressed him as Mr. Trump. There is no greater sign of respect than that. Mr. Trump had a former world champion boxer showing him so much respect. In my opinion Lennox Lewis and Donald Trump got along so well because they are both fighters. Mr. Trump fought his tail off to get back on top of the world, and he did that. He made his life better.

It can get better and it will get better if you believe in yourself and take time to ask God for your inspiration and guidance. If you are having anxiety or depression, please get help now. There are some great doctors and therapists out there that can help you and get you back on track to greatness. Don't go through your bouts alone. You may need a little medicine, but who cares. Look up the top selling drugs each year and you will see that you aren't alone. If you need an antidepressant or anxiety pill, go get it. Find those around who you care about you and talk to them. Speak to those people who survived the late 1970s when it also looked so bleak and you couldn't even buy gasoline. I remember waiting in long lines and watching my parents count change to fill the tank a quarter of the way to get us around.

I think people like to talk more about Muhammad Ali's comeback than when he defeated Sonny Liston for the title the first time. Why is that? We love comebacks. America craves a great comeback or a Cinderella story. Create your own story, sit back, and in five years cherish it. Cherish your family all of the days. There were so many times I was rejected that I began looking for the towel so I could throw it in.

I have personally suffered more pain and anxiety in the last two years than I have in my whole life. There were times I felt like Chris Farley in Tommy Boy. "You don't want to do business with me"? No. "Okay thanks for your time." What can you do? You must persevere and find your inner strength to combat it. Please look around at some of the people who are doing well right now and enjoying life. Ask yourself this question. What do they have that you don't? Not much I'm sure. Imitate those people who are winners and get yourself out of this rut. Watch the Big Idea on CNBC. There are people like you and I on it each night that are living the American Dream because they had a dream and acted on it.

Act out your dream now. Please don't create a nightmare by doing something awful to yourself. I can see how someone could do something terrible to themselves in these conditions. I am not condoning what this man did by ending his own life, but I can actually see why he did it. It is so difficult to feel as though you can't provide for your family and you are worthless. I had many sleepless nights and, as I said earlier, my health has certainly suffered due to the stress of life.

I have worked since I was a young boy. I have told

family members over and over all I want to do is work. I wanted to be slightly successful and come home and worry-free. Well, I was not alone in this idea and, unfortunately, so many people are in the same boat. What do we do about it? We go on and keep trying. The Catholic Church considers suicide a sin. It is a sin to waste your life or give up due to a few bad years. As I said earlier, America loves comeback stories or stories about those overcoming huge odds to win.

Think about Rick Ankiel of the St. Louis Cardinals. He was a pitcher with a strong arm. He developed a problem where he couldn't find home plate with his pitches. He was made fun of by all the sports shows and it made me feel so bad for him. He was sent to the minor leagues where everyone thought, including me, he would be out of baseball in no time. Instead, he switched to the outfield, developed his skills, and is now a successful big leaguer. I have never met him and probably never will, but I can say this to him. You are a role model. Yes I know he had a bad drug test recently. We all make mistakes in life. Rick, please don't do it again. I want to mention you as a success, not a cheat.

Don't cheat your family out of a life they deserve. Fight like Rick. Make a switch and become an instant winner. In my opinion, if Rick Ankiel never plays another game, he is still a winner and someone who should be recognized for perseverance. He needed to get away from pitching, not baseball. Change can be a great thing.

My Girls

Chapter 23

My Church has about twenty thousand parishioners. In fact, it is the largest congregation of any religion in the state of North Carolina. Within the last two years ,we have had three children under the age of ten killed by one of their own parents. This has been such an eye opening tragedy for me. I'm sure that these parents were great at one point and something inside of them snapped. I am not a doctor or a therapist, but I'm sure these people had some form of stress in their life. It is events like these that make me look at Katie in a whole different light.

As I said earlier, if you aren't physically healthy, get to a doctor. Well, if you aren't right mentally, the same rule applies. I know that in 2006 and 2007, I had moments where chaos was taking over my normally pleasant personality. I didn't get help, but I did help myself. I got out of the industry that was causing my inner chaos. These tragedies could have happened in New York, Los Angeles, or Moscow, and they are still tragedies. It doesn't matter where they happen. The fact is, they shouldn't happen. Those little girls should be alive now and there should be two brothers playing right now. The surviving brother shouldn't be blind because his daddy shot him.

Examine yourself and make sure you can handle life's pressures. Pressure doesn't discriminate, and it seems to me that pressure comes in bunches. I love a day when I am stress free, but ask yourself how many days are totally stress free. It isn't what happens to you in life; it is how you respond to it. Respond to life's challenges, but remember you aren't alone. Speak to a loved one, a friend, or a member of the clergy when you think enough is enough. So many people have gone through what you are currently going through. There are good times coming behind the bad times.

So many people tried to ruin Katie's coming into the world party. First, there was a bad doctor. Then, there was a cord around her neck, and lastly a foolish loan officer looking for more money. All of these events could have caused me to become angry or lose the joy in the moment. The one thing these idiots couldn't overcome was my love for that little bundle of joy. Against the odds, she made it and ever since we make every day a great one. I know that next week I have tons of meetings, phone calls to make, and business to find. I know that I have a goal to hit and lots of bills to pay. I know that my stress will increase and I will feel overwhelmed. I also know that my phone will ring at 5:00 and my girls will call me. They will make me laugh and I will hear Kelly yell at Katie as she steals her car keys. That will cause my love to grow and my heart to grow fonder. Stress, you will have to wait 'til tomorrow. Thank you for your patience.

If you still feel your job is too stressful or you can't take it anymore, consider this. There were two Charlotte police officers responding to a domestic abuse phone call one year ago. Both men had families and were very well-respected police officers. A person not involved with the criminal complaint approached them from behind and shot them both dead. For no reason, Charlotte lost two great police officers. More important, two families lost their husbands and their fathers. One officer had a pregnant wife. And you thought your job was too tough? Nothing compares to the grief that these two families share.

As I watched the funeral, I saw the pain on the families' faces as these two men lay in their final resting coffins. Both were taken at least forty years too young. I ask God to pray for these two widows and their children often. I hope these kids make it big in life and never forget that their fathers were both heroes. I can't let Katie feel any pain like that ever. That's why life now has a whole new reason. The pain that these two families experienced helped me realize that life is way too short and way too precious to ever take for granted. Officer Clark and Officer Shelton, I will make a contribution to your children's college fund the way both of you contributed to keeping Charlotte a safer city. Thank you both for your heroism. I hope you both rest in peace. You have also made me realize that my job or jobs never require me to put my life on the line each day.

Chapter 24

I love you Katie. You are my light and my purpose. I have a better understanding through my life experiences what work is all about. I want to enjoy what I do and be the best at it. I don't want to be a statistic like my father. I want to enjoy my life and enjoy all of the days with you. I want to be around for all of your important days. There are so many things I want to teach you as you mature. I have already thought about the speeches I will give when you graduate high school, college, and on your wedding day.

My father wasn't at my wedding or your birth. That still hurts and haunts me 'til this day. My father would have adored you as all of your living family members do. I need to be around for those treasured events. If the good lord blesses me with longevity, I will be in attendance. You came into my life when I needed you the most. You are beautiful, adorable, and an inspiration. You came into the world when my stress was about to erupt like a volcano. Before you came into the world, my sales numbers were such a high priority. Now, your health and your happiness are my priorities. When you entered the world, it was the greatest event I have ever witnessed. Now I want you to witness your Daddy defying the odds and being a great small business owner.

Don't they say four out of five businesses fail? I feel sorry for the other four guys because mine won't. It can't. I will give the best instruction and take care of my clients as if they were my own Katie. If I care about your child as much as I care about Katie, your child is lucky. I know how lucky I am to have Katie in my life. I was heading down the same road as my father until I saw her for the first time. When I saw those blue eyes, Mohawk, and little hands, I knew I had to change. The change from stressed out salesperson to loving father was instinctive. I saw you and I melted. When I held you, I just couldn't put you down. What I did put down was the cell phone and the belief that life is all about sales numbers and re-sults. The result that matters most is how good of a father I am to the girl who saved my life. That will be the true measure of me as a man. I used to measure myself by how many objects I owned, where I bought my clothes, and how much money I made. Now I know that the correct measure is how many smiles I can bring to my girl's face.

Girl, you saved my life. Kelly, please don't change. I love you just the way you are.

For those of you at home right now that are scared, confused, and hurting, I want you to know if I did it, you can do it. You are not alone. Reach deep down inside and look for strength. Get out that pad and paper and write down all of the goals you want to accomplish. It is never too late to have new goals in life. Be your own person, be your own boss, but above all things, love those around you and love yourself. Find your inner strengths now. They are there. God blessed us all with abilities. Half the battle is finding them.

I met a special young man at the YMCA named Sam Milton. Sam is 11 years old and a good athlete. Sam also carries battle scars that no 11 year old should carry. Sam has battled brain cancer for the last few years. The only way you can tell he has battled it is because he has some scars on his head. Sam has an attitude that makes you proud to be around him or know him. I am so proud to have been his coach. The funny thing is I learned more about life, perseverance, and laughter from him than I have learned from anyone. These are the kinds of people you meet at places like the YMCA. I pray for Sam each night. I pray for Sam out of selfish reasons. We need people like Sam around to show us to never feel sorry for ourselves and always have a great smile on your face. I can't wait to have our second child and be a great father. But most of all, I can't wait for tomorrow because Katie and Kelly will be there and whatever we do, we will all do it together.

My girls came into my life at the time I needed them the most. They saved me from making bad choices and being eaten alive by stress. My girls saved my life by being themselves and making me smile each day. The money, jobs, nice things, they all come secondary to a great night in the Cunningham house.

God bless you and keep you all.

About the Author

John Cunningham is a first time author who never planned on being an author. John wrote this book to his wife and daugghter but finally decided to share it with anyone who wanted to read it.